In His Name,

The Lord is our Healer

BY THE SAME AUTHOR

A REPORTER FINDS GOD

GOD CAN HEAL YOU NOW

The Lord is our Healer

by Emily Gardiner Neal

Prentice-Hall, Inc.
Englewood Cliffs,
New Jersey

Library of Congress Catalogue Card Number:
61-16715

Printed in the United States of America
54068-T

Fifth printing......March, 1971

"For by thy words thou shalt be justified, and by thy words thou shalt be condemned." (Matt. 12:37)

THE DEDICATION REMAINS FOREVER UNCHANGED: TO MY HUSBAND ALVIN WILLARD NEAL, AND FOR THE GLORY OF GOD.

TABLE OF CONTENTS

Chapter 1

"confirming the word"

Mark 16:20

A certain bitter-cold night in February will be forever circled in the calendar of my life—the night I inadvertently stumbled upon the fact of spiritual healing.

My initial reaction to that first accidentally attended healing service was not surprising. As an agnostic I was totally unbelieving of its basic premise; as a scientific reporter I was completely skeptical of the "miraculous"; but as a writer, although suspicious of anything which smacked of "faith healing," my curiosity was titillated to the point of investigating what held the promise of a good "story." When after several years of meticulous research and exhaustive study of the Christian Faith, I found the ministry of healing valid theologically, and its results verifiable, scientifically, I thought it the most exciting story I had ever encountered.

My sense of excitement has continued to increase. Today, two books on the subject later, and after four years of extensive travelling where I have been inestimably privileged to observe the healing power of God at work in churches of every denomination, I feel far more than excitement over the marvellous manifestations of the mercy and power of God. For reasons which I shall endeavor to point out throughout this book, the healing ministry seems to me as a layman, as an American, and above all as a Christian, one of the most compellingly important subjects in the world.

Through today's ministry of healing, we see before our eyes spirits recreated, lives regenerated and bodies made miraculously whole. Through it we have demonstrated for us the unique power of the Christian Faith when fully embraced and wholly believed; we have irrefutable evidence for those who need it, and they are many, that God does indeed live and care. There are obviously those who believe without this evidence, as there are those who undergo conversion without this proof; but for each of those who accept Christ through the Church's conventional channels, there are a hundred more who, because of the healing ministry, give themselves to Him.

Most of you who read this book will know far more of spiritual healing than I did when it first came to my attention. I thought then that I had happened on to something new and revolutionary, but I was to discover that the healing ministry is one of the Church's oldest and most dynamic ministries. Jesus mediated His healing power to the Church through His apostles, and the early post-apostolic church, obeying His injunction, "As ye go, preach—heal the sick" (Matt. 10:7, 8), was a healing Church. Physical healings, regarded as part of Our Lord's redemptive process, were expected, and they occurred in large number for several centuries after Christ. Today, through the current world-wide revival of this ministry for so long abandoned by the organized Church, we are witnessing miracles of healing which transcend in wonder anything the Christian world has known since the third century.

The earthly ministry of Our Lord would seem to leave us in no doubt that the curing of physical disease was part of His ministry of salvation; and that whereas the healing of the spirit is of primary and overwhelming importance, it is not the *only* importance—for as total health is never purely a physical condition, neither is it solely a spiritual state. The mission of Christ was at once to redeem the spirit and save the instrument through which it is expressed—the body. It is this mission which the healing Church is continuing today in His Name, by the power of the Holy Spirit.

My first book on spiritual healing presents the evidence and the intellectual process which led me, by means of human conviction, from agnosticism into faith. The second is the story of what I had seen up to that time, and of what I had learned from widespread observation, regarding the healing power of God. This book is in a very real sense a more intensely personal witness than either of the other two, for it stems not only from intellectual conviction and emotional acceptance, but is deeply rooted in personal experience in a realm which, until a relatively short while ago, was not only totally unknown, but basically alien to me. It is written, not as were the other two, primarily for the skeptic, but for the believer. Obviously much must be left unsaid, but the skeptic will not note the omissions, and the believer will read between the lines.

Until very recently, I had no intention of writing this book at this time; first, because the things of the spirit seem to me peculiarly personal, and I had no desire to do a spiritual striptease for public consumption; second, I felt myself a neophyte —a "stranger in a strange land" in the field of the spirit; third, although I have come to see that all Christian experience is in reality a synthesis of personal experience, I have become increasingly alert to the danger of mistaking subjective experience for immutable and universally applicable truth, when the fact is that in many areas the response of each individual is as different as the degree of his understanding. Lastly, I am well aware that whatever effectiveness I have been privileged to exert in my association with the healing ministry, has been due to the fact that I originally approached it as a complete skeptic, and therefore could be objective and dispassionate in my appraisal of the subject.

Some months ago I suddenly realized that I had been fooling myself for several years. I was forced to admit that it was

impossible to be either wholly objective or entirely dispassionate—for one cannot be "objective" about religious conviction,
which is the most subjective of all experiences, nor dispassionate about one's relationship with God.

Why, then, have I decided to undertake this book? Perhaps
it was because the multitudinous cries for help which came my
way each day, thundered in my heart and mind continually, no
matter how arduously I tried to turn my attention elsewhere.
Perhaps it was the man who made a long trip from another
state to tell me personally how the concept of the healing
Christ had changed his life, and his plea for another book on
the subject. Perhaps it was because of the thirteen letters, all
from clergymen, which arrived within a single four-day period
when I was attempting to complete another writing assign-
ment. Each of these letters made substantially the same request: that in my "next" book certain aspects of the healing
ministry be enlarged upon, and certain questions fully dis-
cussed.

It was when I realized that between them, my correspond-
ents had unwittingly outlined a book; it was when I could
honestly conclude that neither my honesty nor my intellectual
integrity need be impaired by my lack of detachment, that I
decided to go ahead. I might say that I have been as assiduous
in acquiring medical verification for the healings mentioned
here, as I ever was in the preceding two books. This is not,
frankly, because I am particularly interested now in medical
substantiation, but simply because of my over-riding fear that
the entire ministry of healing can be discredited by spurious or
hysterical claims of healing.

Many people have asked me if my earlier concepts of spiritual healing have changed. The most accurate answer is probably to say that my *attitude* rather than my concepts has
altered.

I hope and believe that I have learned. I have never deviated
from my first-stated conviction as a Christian, that faith and

the intellect are neither wholly incompatible or totally irreconcilable; that faith does not betray reason but merely goes one
step beyond. Nor have I deviated from my conviction that although faith can indeed be a higher faculty than reason, it
should never be so weakly grounded as to crumble under the
assaults of the mind. Yet only now have I fully understood that
spiritual things cannot be truly discerned by the mind or even
by the heart: that neither the mind's knowledge nor the heart's
persuasion can even dimly perceive those truths which are of
the spirit, and which can be imparted only *by* the Spirit.

I have learned that there is a vast difference between "finding" God and knowing Him—for "finding" is only the first
step. By this I mean that with the mind one can approve the
Christian ethos, and with the heart one can accept God; but
it is only through the grace of the Holy Spirit that one can
receive Him—and immediately this happens, everything else
fades into insignificance and becomes strangely irrelevant.

Above all, I have learned how little I know, and the prayer
now most constantly in my heart and on my lips, is: "That
which I see not teach Thou me" (Job 34:32).

As for changes of attitude: although I never cease to marvel
at the manifestations of God's healing power; of seeing with
my own eyes a tumor dissolve, or a compound fracture instantly
healed, I have in a sense become accustomed to physical healings. That is to say that I have learned to expect them, so that
although they always amaze me, they no longer take me by
surprise. But I have never, and know now that I never shall,
become in any way accustomed to the healings of the spirit I
have witnessed. In them I see, more clearly than ever before,
the incontrovertible evidence of the Holy Spirit at work; the
undeniable proof that God lives.

This past summer, for example, I attended a healing service.
I saw a man deaf for eighteen years suddenly regain his hearing. I saw the clubfoot of a baby straighten before my eyes; a
third-degree burn instantly healed. Now these things and the

many others like them are wonderful to behold, but that day I was to see something which seemed to me even more wonderful.

Kneeling beside me was a woman whose eyes I happened to catch. I think I have never seen such bare, unalloyed misery as was reflected there. Although I had gone to that particular service to pray for someone else, I couldn't help but concentrate my prayers on the woman beside me. When we arose to leave, I saw that tears were streaming down her face. She stopped me in the vestibule on the way out, telling me that she had never before attended a healing service, and that ever since the death of her year-old baby twelve months before, she had been consumed by resentment and bitterness which had made life for her husband—as griefstricken as she at their tragedy—intolerable.

"Sitting in my pew before the service began," she went on to say, "I looked around and spied a small, badly crippled boy. When the service started I felt strongly impelled to pray for this child, and as I prayed, the strangest thing happened. My own bitterness seemed to dissolve and flow out of me like water."

As she told me this, she smiled, alight with that glow which is characteristic of those who have known the healing Christ. As we parted I thanked God, for those haunted eyes were now serene.

I saw this woman and her husband not long ago. He said to me: "I thought I'd never believe in God again—not only because Susan had died, but because of what her death had done to my wife. But through the healing ministry I have come to believe in God as I never could before. Our Lord has healed the wound, and in the healing, both our lives have been completely changed."

In my work in this ministry I have watched people with something akin to awe, as with Herculean effort they strive to move out of evil into good. I have seen them struggle out of ignorance into a daring awareness of the purposes of God—and again and again I have seen Him honor their courage and bless their efforts to reach Him. I have witnessed all manner of diseases healed by His power, and each time I have marvelled as I did a few weeks ago at the healing of a man suffering from a kidney tumor clearly discernible in a series of X-rays. Stating that such a tumor is malignant, or invariably becomes so, the urologist scheduled surgery. Many prayers had been offered for healing, and when the patient was incised, the surgeon found that the operation had already been performed by the Master Surgeon. All that remained was scar tissue. Quick, powerful and sharper than any scalpel, the "Sword of the Spirit, which is the word of God" (Eph. 6:17), had effected the successful operation.

And yet, not long ago I was privileged to witness with my physical senses a healing of the spirit which seemed to me even more remarkable, although the physical results were not dramatic, and I know nothing now of the case other than that the patient is back at work.

It was one day last summer that I was asked to visit a man suffering from an incurable disease whose doctor had predicted he could not live out the week.

I found him in an oxygen tent from which he was removed during my visit with him. Fortunately he had a clear understanding of the healing ministry and a great deal of faith, for I dared talk with him for only a moment, his color was so bad and his pulse so weak.

I laid on hands and began to pray, and suddenly in the middle of the prayer there was such an awareness of the Presence of Christ that I couldn't continue. I glanced at the patient, and was awe-struck at what met my eyes. It was as if I could visibly see the Holy Spirit "stir up," as Paul puts it, the gift of God, which is in each one of us (2 Tim. 1:6). I could see the Hand of God literally mould, before my eyes, this man's spirit.

I saw the tears begin to flow down his cheeks, and watched the color slowly flood his face. This whole episode must have taken place in less than sixty seconds, yet it seemed a lifetime. I knelt by his bed, then took the patient's pulse. It was strong and steady.

He turned to me with the most extraordinary look of radiance, and said very quietly: "Today I have known God. Thank you for bringing Him to me." As he spoke there flashed through my mind the lovely words of John Donne: "I shall not live 'til I see God; and when I have seen Him, I shall never die."

To the believer no explanation of such an experience is necessary. To the skeptic, none is possible.

A few months ago I prevailed upon a physicist I know to accompany me to a healing service. There we saw a young boy dramatically healed of osteomyelitis. The bones of his leg were apparently hopelessly degenerated by the disease. He had been on crutches for a long time, and his bad leg was visibly shrunken from disuse. Before our eyes the limb appeared to expand and assume a normal appearance, and the boy walked unaided.

When a few days later we received via X-ray, corroboration of this healing, my physicist friend remarked: "This sort of thing is going to cause us to make some drastic revisions in our scientific thinking."

His comment recalled Einstein's reply when someone asked him how he came to discover the theory of relativity. "By challenging an axiom," he said.

A number of physicists are now beginning to challenge some basic axioms. They are unanimous in their emphasis that these healing phenomena in no way involve the breaking of certain immutable scientific laws, such as gravity, but are apparently due to the operation of a higher law of which little is yet known.

Since the beginning, I have felt it vitally important to convince the medical profession of the validity of the healing ministry, so that more doctors will cooperate with the clergy in the healing of the whole man—body, mind and spirit. I used to believe that doctors could only be so convinced by concrete medical evidence; and indeed many have, such as the surgeon who operated on a woman for abdominal cancer, which he found so metastasized that removal of the growth was impossible. "Her maximal life expectancy at that time," he said to me recently, "was six months. When she walked into my office four years later, hale and hearty, to show me the result of God's healing power released by prayer, I nearly fainted!"

But while a number of physicians have been startled and impressed by similar instances of divine healing, I have come to believe that many skeptical members of the medical profession may be as well convinced by witnessing a spiritual experience in their patients.

Take the case of a desperately ill man whom I visited at his wife's request. I happened to arrive at the exact same moment as the man's doctor, which at the moment seemed to me peculiarly bad timing, but it was to turn out otherwise.

When I was introduced to the physician, I could feel his hostility assault me. He stated briefly and antagonistically that he had heard of the healing ministry, but obviously any alleged healings must be either psychosomatic or due to original misdiagnosis. He proceeded to examine the patient, then during my visit with the sick man, he waited in another room. As I was putting on my coat to leave, he returned to the sick-room, and about ten minutes later we left the house as we had come, together. As we shook hands in parting, he said: "Medically-speaking, that man should live only a few weeks, yet I have never felt such a strange peace and joy in any human being as I felt in him just now. I must confess that I am more profoundly shaken than I like to admit. What is this thing he has, anyway?"

"God," was the only reply I could make.

The healing ministry has brought many, as it has brought me, nearer to God than we should otherwise have come. It is through it that for me and for many, initial skepticism has gradually changed to intuitive acceptance of certain facts which have finally become personally experienced truths.

As my faith in, and love for God have increased; as the fervency of my belief in the healing Christ has continued to grow; I feel a greater significance and a deeper implication in the present revival of the ministry of healing than I have known before.

I see this ministry not as a *goal*, but as a stepping stone to a greater love of God, a closer knowledge of His Son and a clearer comprehension of the Faith: the lamp which floods with unprecedented clarity *all* the ministries of His Church.

The primary purpose of the ministry of healing is a close relationship with God. Yet I see now that it is *through*, but not *by*, this ministry that we may attain the Kingdom. For the importance of the healing ministry lies not in itself, but in its conversion power, which brings people to God, and in His saving grace, which restores to our churches the incalculable power of the Holy Spirit.

My conviction that God wills healthy bodies as well as redeemed souls, grows daily. And while Christ was not crucified to cure your cold or heal my headache, through His healing miracles we have indeed had "The Word confirmed with signs" (Matt. 16:20).

I have watched and rejoiced over the increasing effectiveness of the healing ministry as little by little we learn more of the spiritual laws involved. But although I am convinced that our redemption of body and soul depends on our efforts to find the answers, I think that we shall never on this earth find them all; for "Man will not find out the work that God has done from the beginning to the end" (Ecclesiasticus). Yet our ignorance, however vast, will from now on be offset by our knowledge, however limited; for God has already revealed enough of His truth to give us certainty when we commit our lives to Him. He has already given us sufficient knowledge that we may recognize Him as He has recognized us. I believe that we must ceaselessly aspire to apprehend His *ways*, but I have discovered that to attempt to analyse *Him* is a form of surgery which can amputate His power and may well sever us from His Life.

We are standing now on the threshold of a new era into which we are being ushered by one of the most curious paradoxes in history. We are living in one of the most highly materialistic civilizations the world has ever known; yet never before has spiritual research been conducted on so impressive a scale. We are living in the greatest scientific age of all time; yet not since Pentecost has the power of the Holy Spirit been more incontestably manifested.

Through the healing Church, which is at once the reservoir of His healing grace, the channel for His healing power and the promulgator of the living Christ, I and thousands like me have first found, and then experienced, God. Through the healing ministry, my life and countless others have been profoundly changed. I have come to know with a clearer vision and a deeper certainty than I have ever known before, the supreme importance of this ministry. It is not merely because through it I have seen the sick take up their beds and the lame walk, although the importance of this should never be underestimated, but it is above all else because I have seen the ears of the spiritually deaf (myself so long among them) unstopped, that they might hear the Word; and the eyes of the spiritually blind (as I for so long was) opened, that they might see the signs.

Chapter 2

why now?

Several months ago I received a letter from a young man preparing his master's thesis on the subject of the current revival of the healing ministry. "Why," he asked, "do you think that this revival is occurring at this precise and seemingly unlikely time, right in the middle of the atomic age?"

My answer is simple: I can't conceive of a *better* time for such a rebirth of spiritual healing to take place, for never have things on this earth been in worse shape, and never has the Christian Faith been more seriously challenged.

"Again and again, when the fires of the institutional Church burned low," writes the Rev. Samuel Shoemaker, "the Holy Spirit has blown upon the embers and recalled the Church to its first vision."* And so it is today. I believe the renascence of the healing ministry is the answer of the Holy Spirit both to the antichrist of communism and its abettor, our own Christian complacency.

We are still ahead of Russia militarily and economically, but a relative handful of communists is jeopardizing, by reason of our lethargy, the faith of 900 million Christians.

I think we mistake the character of the Cold War if we regard it solely as a conflict between two politico-socio-economic ideologies. It is this, too, but for the Christian it is above all a war against the antichrist.

* *With the Holy Spirit and with Fire*, Harper and Bros.

No military defense system, however adequate, can of itself defend us against this enemy; only the "whole armour of God" (Eph. 6:11).

No number of missiles, however superior, can assure us conquest of this aggressor; for it is only "through Him that loved us that we can be more than conquerors" (Rom. 8:37).

It is not the release of hydrogen bombs which will gain the ultimate victory, but the release of spiritual resources, to which we are heirs through Christ. The healing ministry has opened the way to a return to our once power-filled heritage. Through this ministry God has placed in our hands the one weapon against which the antichrist cannot survive. He has given us the greatest instrument of conversion the world has known since the time of Our Lord.

Episcopal Bishop Voegli of Haiti voices a common experience when he says: "Physical healing is the principal means of bringing our pagan hill-billies to God, where they see with their own eyes the power of God victoriously pitted against the voodoo priests."

But we and the entire Christian world have to contend with far more potent adversaries of the faith than voodoo priests; namely those henchmen of the antichrist, our own doubt and indifference. It is today's thrilling manifestations of God's healing power which is overcoming these antagonists by igniting the embers of a largely lip-service Christianity into the blazing faith it used to be. The triumph of Christianity depends on more than the conversion of pagans. It depends on the conversion of nominal Christians to the living Christ. God, through the Holy Spirit, has given us the antidote to apathy.

Not long ago a man crippled by a congenital hip dislocation was inveigled by his wife into attending a healing service. As he knelt at the altar rail to receive the laying on of hands, a sharp cracking noise resounded through the church. This was the moment of his healing—both spiritual and physical.

"I used to call myself a Christian," he said later, "but the truth was I didn't know what I believed, and I cared less. I went to church most Sundays and led a normally decent life, and as far as I was concerned, that was it."

Christians have no monopoly on "decency" and this man like so many others, including myself for many years, had used the term "Christian" not to signify his faith, but only to differentiate himself from a Jew or a Mohammedan or a Buddhist. But today he is a far cry from a merely nominal Christian. On fire with a vibrant and now knowledgeable faith, his witness to the living Christ has influenced hundreds of lives.

"Because thou art lukewarm," said Our Lord, "and neither cold nor hot, I will spue thee out of my mouth" (Rev. 3:16). Indifference can be as damaging to the faith as unbelief; and the lukewarm Christian, basking in a specious security, convinced that he has already "arrived" spiritually, is often harder to jar out of his complacency than the frank unbeliever out of his unbelief. The latter, starting from scratch, is at least open to conversion.

Take the case of a young atheist suffering from a bleeding duodenal ulcer who reluctantly accompanied his mother-in-law to a healing service. "I fought against going," he said, "but it seemed the better part of wisdom to keep the peace with my in-laws."

As an unbeliever he did not receive the laying on of hands; "But in the middle of the healing prayer," he reports, "I felt the most extraordinary sense of some Presence beside me. I was puzzled; then suddenly it came to me in a flash. 'This must be God.' And just then I felt a searing heat across my diaphragm."

This man was healed that day. He is now studying for the ministry.

The communists deride religion as an "opiate for the masses." Perhaps their derision should not anger so much as concern us, for if we are to be strictly honest, we must admit that there is an element of truth in what they say, and the fault is ours. We who are Christians in the largest predominantly Christian nation in the world, have conspicuously failed to demonstrate the vigor and the strength and the power of the faith we profess to hold.

"Let your Yes be Yes, and your No, No," said Jesus (Mark 5:37). It may well be that the militant atheist who has studied religion and found the premise for God unacceptable, is no further from Him than the self-sufficient agnostic ostensibly satisfied with the status quo; and it may well be that both of these are nearer to Him than the unthinking sentimentalist who leans on his religion as a crutch, instead of traversing it as a Way; who uses it as a narcotic to dull the senses rather than a stimulant to revive the spirit; who seeks a kind of limbo rather than the Kingdom, because the road is less rugged.

Recently a woman said to me, a trifle self-righteously, I thought: "I'm devoting my major prayer efforts to the conversion of Russia. Aren't you?"

I had to answer, "No." I pray, of course, for the Soviet Union, but mostly I pray for ourselves. The heavens are flooded with prayers for Russia's conversion, but a tantalizing question continually asserts itself, and will not be stilled: "Conversion to *what?*"

A spiritual analgesic? They have morphia.

The doctrine which we preach but so rarely live by, of a Man who died twenty centuries ago? They have Marx.

The Gospel of Someone we call God, but actually seem to regard more as a two-bit philosopher, some of whose teachings we accept when convenient, and the rest reject when it seems expedient? They have Lenin.

A faith which so little influences us that we have in our Christian nation the highest divorce, crime and juvenile delinquency rate in the world; and the highest ratio of mental and emotional illness?

It seems pretty obvious that until *we* better exemplify the fruits of a faith for which we are not only willing to die to preserve, but more important, willing to live to *prove*, that Russia will not be brought to God.

A psychologist investigating some aspects of spiritual healing interviewed scores of people associated with the healing ministry. "What is it," he asked in bewilderment, "that makes these people stand out in any group? What do they possess that the rest of us don't?"

The answer, I think, is a dynamic Christianity; not only an unqualified belief in His teachings, but a passionate faith centered in and irrevocably bound to, the Person of the Incarnate God. Only when it is wholly this, does the faith become a demonstrable and recognizable force.

It is the *power* of Christianity which from the beginning has differentiated it from all other religions—a power noted by even the pagans of the early post-apostolic era. In the ministry of healing today, as in no other of the Church's ministries, have I seen this long-lost spiritual force restored. In those who participate in the healing ministry as among no other group of Christians, have I seen the power of the Holy Spirit made manifest.

This is not to say that spiritual healing is the only road to God, yet those who have travelled it seem in some unfathomable fashion to have glimpsed the Kingdom. The vision is unmistakably mirrored in their eyes and undeniably reflected in their lives.

In talking to hundreds of people all over the nation, I have found few, whether they seek or whether they receive physical healing, who can remain either impervious or indifferent to the intensity of Our Lord's Presence in the healing Church.

Three years ago, for example, a Jewish woman seeking healing for her husband, began to accompany her Christian friend to a weekly healing service. Her husband died, but she is a convert to the Christian faith; a powerful and inspiring witness for the healing Christ. "No one," she says, "can regularly attend healing services and doubt that Christ lives and cares."

A year ago, following a healing service, this woman introduced me to a young Jewish boy. "I have heard that your faith has power," he said, "but I never believed it until now. Tonight I felt the Presence of your Lord, and I know what you mean." This boy, his whole family, and several of his friends are now Christians. A month ago his mother was wonderfully healed.

The influence of the healing ministry is not confined, nor its purpose contained, in your healing or mine. Yet it is through the testimony of our individual healings that the aggregate faith of the Church is immeasurably strengthened; and it is through the rebirth and expansion of a galvanizing faith in the living God, that His saving health may ultimately be made known to all nations (BCP, p. 18).

But our belief in His teachings must be absolute, and our acceptance of Him complete. A partial Christianity is a travesty of the faith.

A woman suffering from a large tumor, who firmly believed in the healing Christ, persuaded her skeptical husband to accompany her to a healing service. When she walked to the altar rail she gave the appearance of advanced pregnancy. When she returned to her pew after the laying on of hands, her abdomen was flat.

When I talked to her husband it was no surprise to find him now a convinced Christian. "I had always believed in Jesus as a teacher," he said to me, "but until my wife's healing I had never believed in Him as the Christ, the Son of God. I guess you might say that I was only half a Christian."

Many of us are "half" Christians in this sense—but the truth is you can't be "half" Christian any more than you can be "half" pregnant. You either are or you aren't.

The great danger of the partial believer, who cloaks himself in the Christian Ethic rather than the Christian Faith, is that in masquerading as the real thing, he is so often mistaken for it. Russia has made this mistake. She has not penetrated his disguise, but she has discerned that his faith is impotent.

It is through spiritual healing that a nominal, half Christianity has stepped from its spectator status on the fringe of life, into its very core, shaping and molding each individual and filling him with the Christ Spirit. Through the healing Christ, the Christian Faith becomes once more an irresistible force which no man-inspired ideology can overcome; a reality before which complacency crumbles and doubt is overwhelmed. Through her ministry of healing, the Church becomes again the vessel of God's incalculable power—an invincible fortress against which the antichrist must hurl himself in vain. As an apathetic Christian world falls trembling to its knees before the power of the Holy Spirit, so must the antichrist bow down before the living God.

But spiritual healing is more than a means of conversion. For innumerable devout Christians it has provided a foretaste of heaven which they had never dared anticipate on this earth. They had *acknowledged* the power of Christ, but had never felt it. They were daily conscious of His love, but they had never seen it in *visible* action. They had *believed* that He lived, but now they knew.

Such a person is a woman of great faith who all her life has been a dedicated Christian. Recently gravely ill in a hospital, she received at her request, and for the first time, the laying on of hands. "I thought I had known the Presence of God before," she said, her face alight, "but never have I known anything like this."

Through prayer alone this woman had known the Presence. Through the healing ministry she literally experienced God. Her life will never again be the same.

People are brought to God in various ways, but through the healing ministry they come in unprecedented number. These are not "off the top of the head" commitments, but true Pauline conversions, profound and permanent; a spiritual revelation whose influence extends far beyond those who are immediately affected.

"If ye have knowledge let others light their candles by it."

By the witness of those who know, the moribund faith in countless hearts surges to new life.

The agnostic, no longer uninterested; the nominal Christian, no longer indifferent; the devout believer, with renewed conviction, kneel side by side in worship.

"Whom say ye that I am?" (Mark 8:29)

In fervent unison their answer rings out around the world: "Thou art the Christ, the Son of the living God."

Obviously the mission of Our Lord was not to exhibit Himself as a circus-like miracle worker; nevertheless, it was not His Word but His miracles which drew the crowds which followed Him. It was not His theology but His power to heal which arrested the interest of learned priests and untutored fishermen alike.

The same was true of the apostles as they healed in His Name: the crowds came, and they listened when they saw the signs (Acts 2:43, 47; Acts 8:6; 14:3, 11) and they were converted. The same situation recurs today. A woman in Michigan, suffering from incurable cancer, recovers. A man in Wisconsin, dumb since birth, speaks. A child in New York, hopelessly crippled by polio, walks. These, many times multiplied, are the "signs and wonders" (Heb. 2:4) Our Lord has given us —the irrefutable evidence that He lives. At long last we listen to His Word, and now having heard, believe; and now believing, experience in our own lives, for all to see, His transfiguring power.

The night is far spent; the day may well be at hand (Rom. 13:12). For the free world these times are critical; for the Christian world they are crucial. God has richly blessed His total ministry to those wholly committed to Him, but conversely, the forces of evil grow increasingly potent. We are helpless without Christ—and our faith is vain if we cannot demonstrate it.

Russia dreams of conquering the world, but we have a greater dream. "And other sheep I have, which are not of this fold; them also I must bring, and they shall hear my voice; and there shall be one fold, and one shepherd" (John 10:16).

Russia has staged a gigantic revolution; yet the good news of man's salvation through Christ remains the greatest revolution the world has ever known.

Russia offers the Communist Manifesto; we offer the Gospel of Our Lord. Russia promises to save humanity through communism; Christ saved men 2,000 years ago by the Cross.

While it is true that communism has jeopardized the world, it is also true that twelve men, filled with the power of their resurrected Lord, once transformed it. Through this same power and a renewed sense of urgency, Christians today, aflame with a great faith, can do the same.

History has placed the U.S. in a unique position of leadership. The ultimate fate of the world may depend upon our extending this leadership into the spiritual field. If we fail to do so, we may well suffer defeat without the launching of a single missile—for "all that is necessary for the triumph of evil is that good [Christian] men do nothing" (Edmund Burke).

General Douglas MacArthur, after signing the Japanese Peace Treaty, remarked: "The problem is now theological." But the revitalization of the faith depends on more than an inert theology.

In a discussion of the great apologetic which he hoped would some day be written, Msgr. Ronald Knox said shortly before his death: "The hardest part of the author's task will be to introduce some human element into natural theology to prove that God *is,* and *what* God is" (*Msgr. Ronald Knox,* Evelyn Waugh, Little, Brown).

More persuasive than any apologetic which could ever be written, are today's manifestations of the healing power of God. Through the healing ministry we see Christian theology come alive. It offers evidential proof that God *is*—and by the very nature of this proof, *what* He is.

"I am come a light into the world, that whosoever believeth on me should not abide in darkness" (John 12:46).

There has always been the Light, however obscured by unbelief; however dimmed by indifference. Today, through the healing Church, it flares anew. Many who have long walked in darkness, see now its glow. Many who have long lived in His shadow, live now in His light.

The other day a woman said to me in lugubrious tones: "Look what the world has come to, just within my lifetime." I could only respond: "But look what God has given the world —also just within your lifetime."

The healing ministry is His merciful answer to those multitudes starving with a hunger which food cannot alleviate; and thirsting with a thirst which water cannot quench. It is His reply to our pervading doubt and dangerous indifference. It is at once His unmatchable weapon and impenetrable armour against the antichrist, which threatens to destroy us all.

Chapter 3

"thy will be done on earth"

Luke 11:2

The basic premise on which the healing ministry rests, is that sickness is *not* the will of God. If you can whole-heartedly accept this premise you are already within reach of His healing Hand. But if you are one of the many who has been taught all your life that sickness is His will, you may find it difficult in the beginning to embrace what seems a radically new concept.

This was the case with a woman, who during a discussion of spiritual healing, asserted in firm tones: "But sickness *must* be the will of God or we wouldn't be sick."

There was not time that night to refute her statement with theological arguments, so at the risk of over-simplifying, I had to be content with submitting for her consideration, two elemental questions: first, as two-thirds of the Gospels are devoted to Our Lord's healing ministry, and it is recorded that He invariably healed wherever He went (Luke 9:11), is it likely to suppose that He worked in defiance of His Father's will? And second, when she or members of her family were ill, did she seek medical care for them?

These questions are important, for they force all of us to re-assess the sincerity of our avowed Christian faith.

If you honestly believe that your sickness is sent by God to spiritually strengthen you, then to be consistent, you must also believe that Jesus was committing an indefensibly unmoral act if He healed the multitudes (Mark 6:53-56) at the expense of their souls.

If you sincerely feel that God wills your sickness, then, if you are a Christian striving to do His will, you must, to be consistent, reject all medical treatment. Your purpose in receiving it is obviously to be healed, and thus you are deliberately working *against* His will as you conceive it to be.

It is a sort of Christian schizophrenia when we profess to believe that sickness is the will of God, and then when it strikes, rush to call the best doctor available. It is in effect living without integrity—splitting our personalities down the middle, with one belief for religious use, and an antithetical one for our secular lives.

We support enormous research projects in every area of disease. We flock to our hospitals for medical and nursing care; yet all the while we piously declare that sickness is God's will. If we *believe* what we say, such a situation must inevitably induce a sub-conscious spiritual conflict, which of itself can lead to physical illness. This conflict is not restricted to the healing area of the faith. As a prominent businessman and active churchman remarked to me: "My ulcer isn't due to my work, but to the moral strife inside me—the desire to be a good Christian and 'turn the other cheek,' and the social necessity of earning a good living for my family. If I 'give him who has taken my coat, my cloak also' (Matt. 5:39, 40), I'll wake up some morning and find he's made off with my business."

This schizophrenic situation is sharply emphasized by our ostensible worship of a "good" God: the "Father of all mercies and the God of all comfort" (2 Cor. 1:3); a Father whose "good pleasure it is to give you the kingdom" (Luke 12:32); a Father "who knoweth what things ye have need of, before ye ask Him" (Matt. 6:8). And yet any catastrophe which befalls us, we glibly and sanctimoniously declare to be the "will of God."

We may not understand pain and suffering, but we *can*

understand the teaching of Jesus regarding it, and in Him lies the final argument. Throughout His earthly ministry, He showed us the will of God in regard to sickness as surely as in regard to sin. He points out for all eternity, the unmistakable correlation between the Kingdom and our wholeness (Luke 10:9). Again and again He commands His apostles to "Preach the Kingdom of God, and heal the sick" (Matt. 10:7, 8).

He points out for all time the origin of disease when He speaks of the sick being "bound by Satan" (Luke 13:10-17), and, in healing, "rebukes" the sickness (Luke 4:38, 39). He leaves us in no doubt, and neither does St. Paul, that disease does not emanate from God, but from Satan (Luke 11:20, 2 Cor. 12:7).

For us, then, to ascribe the devil's will to God, seems at worst blasphemy, and at best an unthinking alibi for something we cannot fully comprehend. It is a violation of the Faith, for it rejects the revelations of Our Lord concerning the nature of God. It denies the very essence of His Fatherhood: His mercy and His compassion.

To attempt to explain the problem of physical suffering by claiming it to be His will, would seem to come perilously close to heresy; for in the assumption that God wills disease, which according to Scripture He regards as evil, lies the unavoidable inference that He is its Author.

The Church has been primarily responsible for the propogation of this inadvertent heresy. The early Church was a healing church, believed as Christ taught, in the will and power of God to heal. It was between the seventh and eleventh centuries, as her spiritual power began to wane and healings diminished, that the Church began her great rationalization process, promulgating the distortion of the faith which taught that God sent disease; and perpetrating the assumption, wholly unsubstantiated by the Gospels, that God chastens those whom He loves (Heb. 12:6) by afflicting them with sickness that they may grow spiritually.

This sort of rationalization was, and is, the easy way out.

When the healing ministry was still new to me, my husband became seriously ill. I wished often in those days that I could really believe that his illness was God's will. It seemed to me then that such a belief would have been comforting and relaxing, giving purpose to his sickness. But search as I might, I could find nothing in the New Testament to justify such wishful thinking. I was forced to conclude what actually I already knew—that Christianity is not an easy Faith, and Our Lord never said it was—and it is no easier in the area of disease than in the realm of sin. It demands that we do not resign ourselves to either, but fight the one as vigorously as the other, convinced that neither is the will of God—and equally convinced that if we fight the good fight, our battle spoils will include His healing as well as His forgiveness.

Some time ago I was deeply involved with the case of a small child, hundreds of miles away, who was dying of cancer. For a period of many weeks her parents, devout Christians to whom the healing ministry was new, telephoned me frequently. As the child's physical condition deteriorated and her suffering increased, I prayed continually, not only for her healing and the strengthening of her parents, but that something I might say when they turned to me might somehow mitigate their anguish.

With unreserved belief in His assurance that "it is not the will of your Father which is in heaven, that one of these little ones should perish" (Matt. 18:14), we had proceeded from the beginning on the basis that the child's terrible illness was not His will, but an evil thing to be fought with every ounce of strength. However as time went on and I knew so well the parents' agony and emotional exhaustion, I began to waver—never in my conviction, but only as to whether they might find rest in resignation and solace in the idea that their child was suffering according to God's will. I was increasingly tormented by the thought that in order to maintain my own integrity, I was withholding from them possible comfort.

I remember well the last night they called, and their description of her by now appalling physical condition. They had turned to me for help, and that night I would have sacrificed far more than my integrity to give it.

I began to tell them that their child's illness must be His will. I swallowed hard, and it was as if a vice had tightened around my throat, choking off my breath as well as my words. I tried again, but no sound came. It was as if a hand had sealed my lips.

I slept not at all that night. I could only pray.

They called early next morning to tell me that the child had died; and a week later I received a letter from them which read: "We shall always be grateful to you for your continued insistence that her dreadful illness was not God's will. Had we been led to think otherwise, we could not have endured her suffering. We would have lived the rest of our lives in bitterness and hate, had we been able to live at all. As it is, we hate only the evil that caused her sickness. We love God as we never have before."

I trembled to think how perilously close I had come, in my desperate effort to comfort, to leaving them comfortless. I learned that day, shamefully late, that no matter what our individual reaction to it, once having glimpsed the truth, there can be no succour in a lie. I learned that day, that when we act apart from the faith, we do indeed sin (Rom. 14:23). Never did it seem so clear, that if we are Christians we must stand on the faith Christ gave us and live by the truth He revealed to us—for it is by this faith alone that we are sustained by His strength; and through this truth only that we can know the full comfort of His compassion.

I remembered this as week after week I talked and prayed with the heartbroken mother of a child completely crippled by polio. I watched this woman slowly drained of her resentment, and gradually refilled with the love of a God whom she could know was merciful. And I saw her son's limbs straighten before my eyes.

I remembered this, when time after time I visited with the distraught parents of a mongoloid child.

Happy and sweet and somehow seeming close to God as do so many mongoloids, he has improved, but is not yet healed. But I have seen his parents journey from a hostile unbelief to an unshakeable faith in a compassionate Father.

I remembered this when across a hospital bed, my eyes met the anguished eyes of the parents of a little girl who lay unconscious, reputedly dying from injuries suffered in an automobile accident.

"But why," her parents whispered in desperate unison, "why does God want her to die before she's even lived?"

"He doesn't," I could answer firmly. "God is not responsible for the accident; He didn't will these injuries, and He doesn't want her to die. Let's pray now that she be healed, *knowing* that it is His will."

Within twenty minutes the child had recovered consciousness. She made a speedy and uneventful recovery.

"But," you protest, "if some die and others recover, doesn't this mean that God wills the healing of some but not all?"

No—this viewpoint seems to me to be again the rationalization of human failure. It is easy enough to attribute failures of physical healing to God's will, but in view of what His Son taught, it seems to me a radical breach of the faith to do so.

Why some are healed and others not, we don't know. It may be due to impediments, conscious or subconscious, about which we still know very little. It may be due to our complete negativism in respect to certain diseases; that we have more faith in disease to kill than God to heal. It may be that the light of God cannot always penetrate the Church's unbelief. No human being is an island, and we all suffer from the world's corporate sin and faithlessness. But whatever the barriers to His healing power, I am wholly certain that they lie with us and never with Him. It is our inability to receive, not His to give.

The idea which I have heard some express that "certain

diseases must await the Resurrection for healing," is only a qualified version of the old heresy—in my opinion an unwarranted and presumptuous assumption. How do they know? Careful investigation has unearthed records of healings of all these specifically mentioned diseases.

I have said many times that I could not love a God whom I believed to capriciously punish His children with sickness. How much less, then, could I love a God who, standing with Finger poised over the sick, would decree: "*You* I will heal—but *you*, writhing in cancer though you may be, I don't choose to heal." Is this the God "Whose property it is always to have mercy" (BCP, p. 32)? But apart from this personal emotional response, is the irrefutable fact that there is no Scriptural evidence to the effect that He willed the healing of some and not of others, and it is on Scripture that we base the healing ministry. Wherever Jesus went during His earthly ministry, He healed "every sickness and disease among the people" (Matt. 9:35). And this was His indisputable commission to the apostles (Luke 9:2); His unequivocal promise to us (John 14:12).

From time to time the subject of Peter Marshall's death is raised. Not long ago a devout Christian submitted that this event was obviously the will of God because of the great influence of Catherine Marshall's books after her husband's death.

"The fact is," he asserted, "We don't know *what* God's will is in regard to sickness and death."

Actually, I think there is no area in which we can be more certain of His will than in healing. If we don't know what it is in regard to disease, then we don't know what it is in regard to evil, and we might as well throw the entire Christian faith out the window.

At the time of Mr. Marshall's first heart attack, neither he nor his wife knew anything of the healing ministry. (Since then she has become a firm believer, and is the first to deny that her husband's death was necessarily God's will.) For whatever reason, he chose to ignore his physical condition and to disregard all medical advice. The final outcome was inevitable.

Now certainly God did not wilfully disease this minister's heart so that his work on earth would be curtailed. To be sure, He converted the tragedy of premature death to good—but this is not at all the same thing as *willing* it. God did not *need* Peter Marshall's death in order that his influence might be extended through his wife's books. However God may *use* evil, He is never *dependent* upon it to accomplish His purposes.

However, although I am convinced that God never wills sickness or violent death, and that no one is intended to die ill, I have not the temerity to suggest that any of us can be unequivocally certain that He *never* wills the death of someone when, regardless of what *we* may think, his work on earth is over.

About a year ago, a fairly young woman said to me in regard to her latest accomplishment: "You know, I honestly feel that with this I have achieved the full purpose of my life."

Obviously a thing of this matter is not for us to decide—but when I heard that she had died suddenly after receiving Communion, apparently in perfect health, I recalled her statement to me. Some would have thought her too young to die—but I believe that it may well have been God's will.

The measure of a life is not its length, but its depth and influence. God has given us a timeless demonstration of this truth in the physical life-span of His only Son.

Nevertheless, I think we never dare *assume* that He wills an early death.

One hundred years ago, in many world-famous lying-in hospitals, one of every three women died of child-bed fever. This was not the will of God, but poor asepsis. Women now bear their children safely. His will was manifested through Dr. Ignaz Semmelweiss.

One hundred years ago, the average man died at the age of

35. This was not the will of God, but medical ignorance. To-day the life-span has nearly doubled. His will is being manifested in medical advancement.

Until recently, thousands of children were crippled by polio. This was not the will of God, but lack of a protective vaccine. Children no longer need be maimed. His will has been manifested through Dr. Jonas Salk.

My unqualified acceptance of the Christian Faith has come neither easily nor quickly, but once having received it, the premise that God wills, and has the power to restore, our wholeness, has been, for me, among the easiest of all its tenets to accept. Believing that God works through men, we see His guiding Hand in the expansion of men's knowledge, by which life is being prolonged and disease eradicated. Believing the teachings of Our Lord, it would seem that such a concept *must* follow as a logical consequence of this faith. That it proves a stumbling block for so many appears to me largely a matter of misapprehension.

Many of us confuse the concept of suffering in the New Testament—a suffering which Our Lord makes clear, derives from persecution rather than sickness; from spiritual conflict rather than disease; from moral struggle rather than physical ailments.

Our joy in the Resurrection must never blind us to the Cross—but as Christians, the Cross for us is a symbol of salvation as well as agony. The lesson of His Passion lies not in the fact that He suffered for pain's sake but for us, that we might be saved. The point of the Crucifixion is not that He died, but that by His death we are assured everlasting life. As our Redeemer, He "took our infirmities and bare our sicknesses" (Matt. 8:17). We cannot imitate His redemptive acts. We can only try to follow Him.

Another common source of confusion is due more to semantics than to theology: the tendency to regard as synonomous, the words *will* and *permit*. That God *wills* disease, is to me, unthinkable. That He *permits* it is self-evident. He permits it

in exactly the same sense as He permits rape and murder and
evil of all kinds. Did He not, our free will would be illusory
and a Redeemer unnecessary. God would have created us voli-
tionless puppets without the capacity to sin.

But if God is all-powerful, why does evil so habitually seem
to over-ride good, and Satan so frequently appear to triumph
over God?

Perhaps because the dramatic effects of evil are more often
startlingly apparent than the unobtrusive consequences of
good. Perhaps because according to God's plan, His omnipo-
tence is not demonstrated by despotically exterminating evil,
but by triumphantly overcoming it. We rest on Christ's assurance that no alien force, however powerful, can prevent the
final fulfillment of His plan for us, which is good. On this
earth His will can be temporarily deflected by human sin and
corporate evil, but in the timelessness of God, it can never be
permanently defeated.

But although neither evil nor disease can frustrate His ultimate purpose, if our bodies are "temples of the Holy Spirit" as
we are told (1 Cor. 6:19), we cannot rationally believe that
God intends them to be at any time contaminated by sickness.
As Jesus' ministry would not have been more effective had He
suffered from tuberculosis, so neither does cancer or arthritis
better fit *us* to serve Him.

Yet if you are sick, but react to your sickness as did the
saints (whose reaction to, not their suffering, determined
their saintliness), offering it to God, He can and will convert it
to His holy use. This we see in true redemptive suffering, where
the sufferer is not the hapless victim of a cruel God, but the
sanctified recipient of His merciful transforming grace. Our
Lord never fails to make crystal clear, however, that "God
does not *willingly* afflict His children" (Lam. 3:33).

For the believing Christian, the ultimate power rests with
God—and the final word with His Son. By mistaking His will
we are, however unintentionally, disclaiming His power and
repudiating His Word.

Chapter 4

"send out thy truth and thy light"

Psalm 43:3

Christianity is a healing religion and Christ a healing Saviour "Who forgiveth all thine iniquities; Who healeth all thy diseases; Who redeemeth thy life from destruction" (Psalm 103:3, 4). He heals all brokenness: broken relationships as well as broken spirits; broken hearts as well as broken bodies. In the overall sense, He came to heal the world, and in this same sense every ministry of the Church is, or should be, a healing ministry.

I who have seen among others, a moribund infant restored to life through Baptism; a polio victim walk through Confirmation; a cancer sufferer cured through Holy Communion, am inclined to concur with a clergyman who says: "Not to accept the *bodily* fruits of the Sacraments as well as the spiritual, is a denial of Christ."

There are those who refer to the healing ministry as a "lay movement," but with this I cannot agree. While it is true that God is manifesting this ministry to a great extent through the laity, it is in my opinion a sacramental ministry in exactly the same sense as all the other ministries of the Church. As such it is a vital and indispensable part of the Church's total ministry, and cannot be dismissed as a mere "movement" whose historical destiny it is to flourish for a few years and then die

out as though it had never been. The healing Christ is eternal
—not a temporary illusion or a transitory enthusiasm.

The Holy Spirit operates in different ways and through various channels, for the Spirit of God "bloweth where it listeth."
But because I am convinced on the authority of Jesus that the healing gift was given by Him, through His apostles, to the Church; because I am so *sure* that His complete healing power resides within the Mystical Body waiting only to be released by faith, I believe that it is His Church which must lead and guide us in this deeply spiritual and enormously difficult ministry. For how can we know the truth if it be not taught us?

The Church's specific ministry of healing embraces those same methods used in the early Church and authorized by Our Lord Himself; the laying on of hands and Holy Unction (anointing with oil). The former, which may be employed by spiritually gifted laymen as well as clergymen, is by far the more familiar rite, being universally used by the healing Church in all its branches. Unction, as a formal Sacrament instituted in the ancient Church explicitly for physical healing (James 5:14), should be administered only by a clergyman and only to those conversant with its intention. If the patient is not instructed, his reaction can be psychologically unfavorable as it was in the case of a man hospitalized for a serious but not dangerous ailment. When the chaplain, who mistakenly believed him familiar with the rite, asked if he would like to be anointed, he flew into a near panic, exclaiming: "I didn't know I was dying!"

As knowledge of the healing ministry has expanded, this connotation with imminent death is less prevalent; and even the modern Roman Catholic Church is now discussing the original use of this Sacrament as a channel for life rather than a preparation for death. Not long ago a Roman priest remarked with commendable forthrightness: "It was the large number of recoveries of desperate illness after receiving Extreme Unction which led me to discover that this Sacrament was not originally intended for the final absolution of the dying, but for the healing of the body."

As clergymen of some denominations are not instructed in the use of this rite, and as most of those who are demand special spiritual preparation of the patient before receiving it, its use is generally limited to private ministration upon request. A personal experience emphasized for me the necessity of this prior preparation.

I had been anointed before, always with spiritual and physical benefit. One day, due to what seemed then unavoidable circumstances, I received Unction—in faith and with prayer to be sure—but without any special previous preparation. I found it if not meaningless, nevertheless an empty and powerless ritual. Since that time it has occurred to me that it is precisely *because* of the spiritual requirements which precede its administration, that it is so singularly valuable to so many who seek healing; but it is the very *necessity* of this painstaking preparation as well as general unfamiliarity with its purpose, which most clergymen feel precludes its uninformed use at public interdenominational healing services. I could wish that the public were more widely instructed in the significance of this Sacrament so that it might be restored to its rightful place in the Church's ministry. As the *specific* rite for bodily healing it is a uniquely valuable instrument; and because of its nature, which involves virtually no physical contact between the officiating minister and the receiving layman, there is less tendency to deify the "healer," and a more ready recognition of Who it is that heals.

I have become convinced that the complete healing ministry as such, must include not only prayer and the healing rites, but also some form of confession (taught by St. James to be an essential accompaniment to Unction and the prayer of faith— James 5:16); and Holy Communion, which in healing as throughout the Church, is indeed the "Sacrament of Consummation."

Any one of these Sacramental Acts when properly understood, has great power. When all three are used in sequence, the result is spiritual dynamite.

"I discovered this purely by accident," a woman told me recently. "I was suffering from profound nervous exhaustion, and had been advised by my neurologist that it would be some months before I could return to my job. I received Unction, preceded by Confession, on a Saturday. I felt better afterwards, but far from well. The next day happened to be Communion Sunday, and although ordered to stay in bed by the doctor, I decided to go to church. It was there, at the altar rail, that I received the full impact of God's healing power—a force so tremendous that for a few seconds I felt I couldn't physically withstand it. And then I was aware of such a surge of vitality as I have never before experienced. Within two days I was back at work, feeling better than I ever had before in my life."

But in this emphasis on the sacramental approach, the importance of the Word should never be overlooked. "He sent His Word and healed them" (Psalm 107:20) is a truth we see demonstrated again and again.

A woman who had been attending healing services for several months says: "The service then consisted solely of prayer and the laying on of hands—which should have been enough, but somehow wasn't. It was not at these services that I felt His healing power, but on a Sunday morning as I listened to a sermon on the Miracles of Our Lord. As a consequence, I was healed of arthritis of the spine."

It was after this that her pastor began to include, as part of each healing service, a brief sermon based on Scripture.

"When I started this healing ministry," he said, "I was groping in the dark, as there is no set format for the service. It was this woman's experience which made me realize anew to what extent 'faith cometh by hearing the Word of God'; and as a result of this faith, I have seen that miracles do indeed occur."

The Holy Spirit came upon each individual apostle; but He came upon them not primarily as individuals, but as members of His Mystical Body. And so it is today. There are many spiritually gifted laymen; and there is now, as there was in the early Church, a vital and definite place for them in the healing ministry, but *only*, I think, if they work within the framework of the Church, under the closest sort of Church supervision. The law in this case will not kill the spirit, but on the contrary, allow it to flourish.

The gifted layman tends to grow impatient with the lagging Church, and chafing under its constraints, is tempted to work independently of it. Although the initial results of this divorce can be dramatically successful, it is frighteningly easy to drift insidiously into various heresies, the greatest of which is to permit physical healing to become an end in itself, rather than God. When this happens, the result is always catastrophic spiritually, and usually disastrous physically.

Take the case of a woman whose husband suffered from a medically incurable disease. She had dabbled in various religions, taking what she wanted from each, and emerging with her own version of God which had little to do with the Judaeo-Christian tradition of faith. She had "no use" for any church, nor did her husband, but she had heard of spiritual healing. "If there's anything to this healing business," she said, "I'm going to see that Jim gets his share of it."

She sought out several so-called Christian healers who worked outside the Church using their own techniques and their own approach. Two of these "promised" that Jim would be healed, so it was to these two that she took him again and again.

When he died, she was filled with so deep a bitterness and resentment that her own health is now virtually destroyed. The last time I saw her, two years after her husband's death, she flung out at me: "Why did that God of yours have to single out *my* husband *not* to heal!" In true spiritual healing within the Church, wherein lies the authority, the control and the Power, this sort of incident cannot occur.

There are many aspects of the one great truth, and to each may be given a small fragment of knowledge; but no individual has it all, only the Church Universal which must be the ultimate organ of revelation.

"The Lord whom you seek will come to His temple" (Mal. 3:1). And because I have seen so many perversions and excesses practiced among genuinely gifted but over-zealous laymen, I am convinced that this ministry cannot survive unless it is both protected and sanctified by the Church.

I believe that, as laymen, everything we do in the healing field, whether witnessing or laying on hands, whether teaching or just believing, should be done with one purpose in mind: the edification of His Church. This was the injunction of St. Paul (1 Cor. 14) and his reasons were probably much the same as ours today.

Many people have questioned me concerning the healing work of the Pentecostal churches. There seems no doubt that more frequent and more dramatic healings take place here than in the established Church. There is in these sects a marvellous intensity of faith, flaming up to a great and wonderful blaze. But historically this flame seems invariably to reach a certain heat, begins gradually to subside, then sputters out altogether. The Pentecostal church is like a meteor, incandescent with faith, which from time to time flashes across the sky to brighten the Church but it is not the Church itself, which is the creation of Pentecost, and which will remain to the end of the world.

We are inclined to be supercilious about the Pentecostal methods; but there seems to be abundant evidence that God honors and confirms truth wherever He finds it, even if it is only a fragmentary truth—a splinter from the whole.

Although it is sometimes difficult to differentiate in the Pentecostal environment, between human commotion and the tumult of the Holy Spirit, those of us who have watched these churches in action cannot, I think, deny His power there— and perhaps wish that there were a little more evidence of it in our own churches, which have for so long striven to do His work without His power.

We are apt to smugly criticize the Pentecostal sects because we say they preach a distorted Gospel, overemphasizing certain aspects of the Faith, such as healing. This is true, but when I see so many of *our* churches preaching only half the Gospel by omitting healing altogether, it seems a moot question whether it is better to *distort* the Gospels or *truncate* them. If we are to demonstrate the truths we profess to hold, we might do well to strive for something of the Pentecostal's simple faith; his intensity of personal experience, and his pervading awareness of the living Saviour; all of which are characteristics of the early Church.

We see these prime requisites of a dynamic faith being recaptured today in the healing Church, which in obedience to His three imperatives to preach, to teach and to *heal* is fulfilling the divine commission. Here, fervor stabilized by discipline, zeal balanced by the preaching of a complete Gospel, and ardor sanctified by the Sacraments, have resulted in a quiet but nonetheless positive outpouring of the Holy Spirit. Through the healing ministry we have learned at last the momentous difference between having the Spirit *in* us and merely *with* us; between *responding* to Him, and *experiencing* Him.

I do not underestimate the difficulties of the ministry of healing. For many, both clergy and laity alike, it means a complete reappraisal of their faith. It means daring to go out on a limb for Christ. It means the end of a nominal Christianity, and the beginning of a discernment that erudition is no substitute for the Holy Ghost; that "faith stands not in the wisdom of men but in the power of God" (1 Cor. 2:5). This ministry is Christianity bare. It means for the administering clergyman, handling the power of God; and for the receiving layman, direct contact with the Holy Spirit Himself. These are awesome things which cannot and should not be undertaken lightly— but they *must* be undertaken, or we stand guilty of His condemnation "that light is come into the world, and men loved darkness rather than light" (John 3:19).

Regardless of our scientific knowledge and our abundance of doctors and hospitals, the need for our churches to become sanctuaries of healing is no less today than in the early post-apostolic era. The centuries have not quelled our hunger for the living God, nor the passing years obviated our need for the healing christ. The extent of that need and hunger among people of the established churches is illustrated by the far from unique report of one diocese. Here, in one year, 3600 new members were received into the Chuch; yet the total growth of membership for that year was only one hundred persons. "This means," said the Bishop, "that 3500 people left the Chuch— and to my personal knowledge, most of these defected to Christian Science or similar healing sects."

In mentioning to me such defection, a Churchman scathingly remarked: "This sect she's joined accepts the *gifts* of Jesus, but doesn't accept *Him*."

But the vast majority of us accept Jesus and reject His gifts. In both cases this seems to me heresy. The difference lies only in degree.

"God is the Lord, which hath showed us light" (Psalm 118:27). Its effulgence irradiates the Church as the Holy Spirit continues to edify.

Not long ago I was called to the home of a reputedly dying man. I had asked that a clergyman be there to administer Holy Communion before the laying on of hands, and he met me at the door. With that wonderful humility I have noted again and again in the Church, he confessed that although he was intellectually convinced of the validity of the healing ministry, he had never seen any direct evidence of the healing power of God. "To be truthful," he said, "my faith in this area is awfully weak, so perhaps it would be better if I did not lay on hands."

He was persuaded otherwise, and after the Communion Service we laid on hands together. During the healing prayer there came such an overwhelming sense of the Presence, that I think even an unbeliever must have acknowledged Him by whatever name he chose to call Him. The power of God was gloriously manifested, and the patient almost literally took up his bed and walked—from death.

But the scope of His healing was not confined to the curing of one individual. It never is. On his knees at the end, the ministering priest had received what he termed, "The greatest spiritual experience of my life." His witness was to set aflame his diocese, and as a result, many healing ministries have been instituted in that locality—led by his own Spirit-filled example.

"While ye have light, believe in the light." (John 12:36) Through this single ministry, guided by the Holy Spirit, it has been made to shine in many hearts, giving knowledge of the glory of God (2 Cor. 4:6).

Benjamin Franklin wrote: "He who shall introduce into public affairs the principles of primitive Christianity, will revolutionize the world."

We have seen through the healing Church the extent to which the faith, and thus eventually the world, can be revolutionized by the re-introduction of the primitive Church's ministry of healing. We have seen unloosed by faith the incalculable power of the Holy Spirit so long shackled with unbelief; and in the restoration of her lost spiritual power, we have seen the Church metamorphosed from the body of men she has too often unworthily become, to the Mystical Body of Christ she is intended to be.

"What has happened to the Christian Church," asks an eminent clergyman, "that it should still so largely relegate His command to heal, to the tents of itinerant evangelists?"

As nearly two-thirds of the Gospels are devoted to Our Lord's healing ministry; as we repeatedly assert as Christians, that Our Lord is the same yesterday, today and forever, and therefore presumably cannot have lost His power to heal any more than to save souls; as the primary purpose of spiritual healing is a closer relationship with God; and as there is an evergrowing number of scientists who are coming to accept the fact that there is in operation an indisputable healing force, some of us can only wonder that every church in Christendom does not practice this ministry.

We remember His words: "Why call ye me Lord, Lord, and do not those things which I say?" (Luke 6:46)—and there reverberates in our brain His command: "Preach ye the Kingdom of God and heal the sick" (Luke 9:2)—an indivisible phrase, unmistakable in intent. Dare we continue to apostasize?

We are told that when the Spirit of Truth is come, He will guide us into all truth (John 16:13). "But how can we believe in Him of whom we have not heard; and how shall we hear without a preacher?" (Rom. 10:14)

E. L. Mascall, British theologian comments: "The notion that religion has as its object the deliverance of our souls from the entanglement of our bodies is a pagan view against which the Christian Church has consistently waged war. Not the deliverance of our souls from our bodies, but the sanctification and the super-naturalization of our whole being—body and soul alike—this is the purpose for which the Church exists."*

"Send out thy light and thy truth that they may lead us," is our plea, then, to the Church. The words spoken by Peter and Paul nearly two thousand years ago to the young Church, is our continual prayer: "And now, Lord, grant to thy servants to speak thy word with all boldness, while thou stretchest forth thy Hand to heal" (Acts 4:29 RSV).

---

* *Grace and Glory*, Morehouse-Barlow, publishers.

Chapter 5

gifts of the spirit

Two thousand years ago the power of the Spirit was poured out upon the Church; and by this power the disciples cast out demons, healed all manner of diseases and raised the dead.

"But that was two thousand years ago," objected a liberal churchman. "What do you expect in our churches today, anyway? The Pentecostal tongues of fire?"

Yes. We not only *expect* these tongues of fire, but in the healing Church we have felt their heat; and we feel in our faces the rushing, mighty wind. Pentecost is no longer solely myth or legend or even history out of the dim past. It is recurring today with many of the same manifestations as twenty centuries ago.

Many of the established churches have long either repudiated or ignored the supernatural, relegating the Gifts of the Spirit to the same category as the Gospel Miracles: phenomena which perhaps occurred in the time of Our Lord, but certainly have no application to us today. However, as we see about us the evidence of charismatic healing; as through the healing Church we are witnessing the "signs and wonders" of the Holy Spirit, as a result of which the "Lord is adding day by day those who would be saved" (Acts 2:43, 47), so also are we witnessing remarkable evidence of other gifts of the Spirit.

One of the most startling manifestations has been the reappearance in the established Church, of glossolalia, or the speaking with tongues. This phenomenon, appearing at the first Pentecost when "they were all filled with the Holy Ghost and began to speak with other tongues as the Spirit gave them utterance," was commonly practiced by the early Christians who regarded it as evidence of the presence of the Holy Spirit.

Recently a veritable bombshell was exploded in the laps of conservative Christians by the widely publicized disclosure that speaking in tongues, long associated primarily with the Pentecostal sects, had suddenly invaded the ultra-dignified and "respectable" Episcopal Church. The news that in some instances both clergy and laity were practicing this phenomenon, was met with no little consternation by the majority of Episcopalians. Coupled with their justifiable fear of overemotionalism, they shared with most members of the organized churches an intense reluctance to be jarred out of a comfortable Christianity by any evidence of the supernatural.

"This whole thing is utter and complete nonsense," exploded an irate churchman. "Good heavens, this is the twentieth century! What *rational* human being could be expected to believe in supernatural 'gifts'?"

I venture to say the same sort of presumably "rational" human beings who profess the Christian Faith—a Faith based on the supernatural from beginning to end: from the Virgin Birth through the Resurrection and Ascension, to the sending of the Holy Ghost (John 14:26).

"Oh, I never *did* believe in the Virgin Birth or things like that," expostulated someone else.

"Do 'things like that' include the Resurrection?" I asked.

"Sure," came the reply. "That wasn't *actual*—just an allegory."

Then indeed we are banking our lives on a superstition and not a Faith—for "if there be no resurrection of the dead, then is Christ not risen. And if Christ be not risen, then is our preaching vain, and your faith is also vain" (1 Cor. 15:13, 14).

"Well, *I* believe in all those things, and Christ's Miracles, too," interpolated another. "But that was centuries ago. Nothing supernatural like that could possibly happen today!"

Did God, then, die for all time in 33 A.D.? And did the operation of the Holy Spirit cease forever before the end of the first century?

The fact that so many of us who claim to be Christians have reduced the Faith to the status of a fairy tale; the fact that so many of us, although we may accept the historicity of Christianity, refuse its revelations, has, not surprisingly, robbed the New Testament of its relevancy and rendered the Faith virtually impotent.

Perhaps the greatest of all testimonies to the mercy of God, is that He has borne with us for so long, and once again is manifesting Himself to those who will see; and bestowing upon those who by faith can receive, His grace.

All of the gifts He has given are rendered that He may be glorified and His Church edified. All can be and often are, misused—and the most subject to abuse is probably the speaking with tongues, which is why its practice should be carefully examined and controlled.

St. Paul says: "I thank my God that I speak with tongues more than you all" (1 Cor. 14:18); but he immediately adds: "Yet in the church I had rather speak five words with my understanding than 10,000 words in an unknown tongue" (1 Cor. 14:19).

Although he considered glossolalia the least of the Gifts, he devotes an entire chapter to it (1 Cor. 14), pointing out its dangers—the same ones which obtain today, and which can be largely obviated if the scriptural safeguards are punctiliously heeded: namely, it should never be used without the accompanying Gift of Interpretation (1 Cor. 14:28); for otherwise it is incomprehensible gibberish which edifies no one (1 Cor. 14:13, 27); and it should be practiced only in *small* groups of the faithful, for "if the whole church assembles and all speak in tongues and outsiders and unbelievers enter, will they not say that you are mad?" (1 Cor. 14:23 RSV)

If these injunctions are obeyed there is little likelihood of exhibitionism or little possibility of the frenzied emotionalism which is characteristic of the practice in the Pentecostal churches.

I have witnessed no excesses of any kind in the vast majority of small groups practising this phenomenon, which are quietly and undeniably in the Spirit. In extremely rare instances, (conspicuously among those which have failed to follow Paul's warning to *interpret*) I have felt that excess ardor and over-eagerness have resulted in human emotionalism which has been genuinely mistaken for the Holy Spirit—but these few exceptions in no way nullify the authenticity of the Gift. The over-riding danger as I have seen it, and the one which must be scrupulously guarded against, is that of spiritual pride—the tendency among some who have this gift, to disparage the quality of the faith of those who have not.

"Forbid not to speak in tongues," adjures St. Paul; "but let all things be done in decency and in order" (1 Cor. 14:39, 40).

It is towards this end that the prelates of the Episcopal Church are working; for although none of us, either clergy or laity, are unaware of the consequences if this grace is injudiciously exercised or permitted to assume disproportionate importance in our spiritual lives, most agree with the Rt. Rev. Austin Pardue, Bishop of Pittsburgh, who comments: "The Church *must* be open to it, and never in the position of rejecting any valid gift of the Spirit."

I can only rejoice that in the Episcopal Church, among its so-called "frozen" people, there is occurring on many fronts a great and wonderful breakthrough of the Holy Spirit. As this Church has taken the lead in the revival of the healing ministry, and in her return to the power-packed truths of Scripture has received a mighty increase of the Holy Ghost, it seems scarcely surprising that other gifts of the Spirit are being manifested.

The other night a woman remarked, "I can see some *reason*

in gifts such as wisdom or knowledge or faith or healing, but what is the *purpose* of speaking in tongues?"

I do not know an intellectually satisfying answer to this question; but I do know that at least one of its purposes might well be to enable us to better magnify God; to express to Him that which we find inexpressible in any language that we know. Beyond this, I know that it is a grace given by the Holy Spirit as a sign to the believer (1 Cor. 14:22); a fulfillment of His promise: "And these signs shall follow them that believe—in My Name they shall speak with new tongues" (Mark 16:17). That it is a gift instituted by Our Lord Himself, would seem enough to make its possession sought and prized.

"Covet earnestly the best gifts," said St. Paul (1 Cor. 12: 31), "and yet show I unto you a more excellent way." This way is love, one of three theological virtues, which although not among the nine gifts enumerated by the apostle, must appear in their midst, for it is their principle, their motive, their reason for being: the chief fruit of the Spirit which leads us *to* the gifts, and without which they are rendered profitless and we destitute.

Not long ago a woman said to me: "We're continually told to love God, but no matter how I try I can't seem to *really* love Him. How can you love someone you don't actually know?" I suspect she was stating a problem which many of us have, but do not so readily admit.

We all know that we should love God because He first loved us (1 John 4:19), but many of us have no personal sense of the reality of His love for us. We try, because we know we should, to *force* ourselves to love Him—but love, unlike worship, can never be an act of the will, but must be an emotional response—and it is virtually impossible to emotionally respond to the concept of a vague Creator of the universe. God knows this which is one of the reasons why He sent us His Son, that we might know and love Him as a Person as well as God.

Through the healing Church we experience so uniquely

vital a confrontation with Christ; we are so certain that He lives and so sure of the actuality of His love, that we are impelled to emotionally respond. This is the love of the heart. When it enjoins the Source of all love, it becomes at once both a power and an absolution.

Obviously the ministry of healing is not the sole purveyor of love any more than it is of faith. Yet it is through those associated with this ministry that I have learned for the first time exactly what Tertullian meant when he said, 1700 years ago: "See how those Christians love one another!"

A prayer group met regularly for some weeks to pray for the healing of a small victim of leukemia. They met in love for God, for one another and for the patient. The child was healed; for although the doctors claim that a cure for this disease is impossible, and what has transpired is only a remission, the so-called "remission" has lasted now for over eleven years.

In speaking of this case to a clergyman, he said: "I don't doubt the healing, but I *do* doubt that any group of people could meet time and again in the sort of love you describe. It is humanly impossible."

Not very long ago I might have agreed—but no longer. Earlier I spoke of the extraordinary illumination or insights which the healing ministry brings in its wake. For me, one of the most wonderful instances of this has dealt with love.

I have always been a normally affectionate and compassionate person, but it wasn't until relatively recently that I had any real concept of the meaning of agapic love. To call this emotion love or charity is the closest we may come, but it's a long way off. It is totally different from anything that I, personally, have ever known. It is not a feeling of affection, or pity or compassion—although it is these too—but rather does it seem to me a force, a power, a grace, which cannot be defined.

The first time I became cognizant of it was about two years ago when I walked into a sick-room. It was an ordinary room, inhabited at that moment by the patient, his wife, and a priest who was preparing to administer Holy Communion before the laying on of hands.

Suddenly, as we knelt in prayer, that room was so filled with love—for lack of a better word—that it defies description. Our love, one for the other, seemed a palpable, viable thing. None of us had ever seen the other before, and most probably would never meet again. Yet each one of us, for those wonderful moments, would have given his life for the other; and as God's transcendent love washed over and into us, each would have fought for the privilege just then of being crucified for Christ. Nothing evil of any sort; no sickness of any kind could have withstood the power of this overwhelming and transfiguring force. A marvellous healing took place that day. It couldn't have been otherwise.

"Love is of God, and everyone that loveth is born of God and knoweth God" (1 John 4:7). It was on that day that I first began to really grasp the enormous significance in these words. It was then that I caught my first vision of what a world lit by the knowledge of the love of God could be.

A short time ago I heard someone remark: "The trouble with the world is that more people love God than love their neighbors."

I question this assertion. Rather would I say that not enough of us love God, and hence we *cannot* love our neighbors."

As God works through men, His love must be expressed through persons. "If we love one another—His love is perfected in us" (1 John 4:12). And yet, or so it has seemed to me, I think we cannot truly love one another until we first love God. It is only as a consequence of *our* love for *Him* that our hearts become wholly receptive to the fullness of *His* love for *us*. It is this which seeks and finds expression in our relationships with other people. All love is of God, who is the God of the atheist as well as the believer; but to love others and not Him is perforce to love with only half our capacity; while to love Him and not others, is an impossibility.

Perhaps it is no accident that His First and great Commandment is: "Thou shalt love the Lord thy God with all thy heart, and with all thy soul, and with all thy mind"; and as a natural corollary, the second follows: "Thou shalt love thy neighbor as thyself."

The Christian Faith teaches us to love humanity, but many of us have only learned to love *man* through the healing ministry.

"For a long time my own healing was all that mattered to me," a woman told me recently, "and for months it was all I prayed for. Then one day a stranger, obviously in pain, knelt beside me at the altar rail. For the first time I completely forgot myself and began to pray for *her*. Strangely enough, I discovered just the other day that we had both been healed within a couple of weeks after that service."

This is love in action—the power of the healing ministry, which, whether we seek healing for ourselves or pray for others, is, or should be, an outpouring of ourselves, which inevitably results in an ingathering of His power. I am increasingly convinced that the reason Christ is so powerfully and abundantly present in the healing Church lies in the fact that so many of those kneeling at the altar rail are filled, if only for a few moments, with compassion and love for someone other than themselves; and concerned however briefly, with something other than their own frustrations. This love and concern, coupled with a singleness of faith, releases the power of God as it is not often otherwise released.

It is in praying for others that many of us first begin to apprehend agapic love, for we find ourselves spiritually bound to those for whom we pray, and although we may have never seen them face to face, we learn to love them with a remarkable profundity.

Still vivid in my memory is the typical example of a young

child in a far-off country for whom I prayed over a period of
many weeks. During this time I came to love him as though
he were my own—and often as I prayed, he became curiously
inseparable in my heart and mind, from my own children. So
close to him did I feel, that many times I felt almost uncertain
as to whose child I was praying for. This is the sort of love
with which we, as individuals, have nothing to do; for it is a
"spark dropped from the Flame which is God" (Fulton
Sheen). Because of its Source, it embodies a healing virtue of
incalculable power, transcending both space and time.

I have discovered that as we learn to pray for others and
really care about them, a curious thing happens: there is
simultaneously born in *us* a new and cogent awareness of the
love of God. Whereas such an awareness was once a momentary, fleeting thing, it now becomes a steady, continuing
consciousness of His love which we feel perpetually pouring
into and through us, transforming everything we think and
do and are.

"Herein is love: not that we loved God, but that He loved
us, and sent His Son to be the propitiation for our sins"
(1 John 4:10). At last we *truly* comprehend the message of the
Cross.

Cardinal John O'Hara said at his installation as Archbishop
at Philadelphia: "I have no program to announce, and nothing
to preach but the love of God." Nothing? This is all any of us
need to know.

"Now concerning spiritual gifts, I would not have you
ignorant," says St. Paul (1 Cor. 12:1).

We are no longer, as throughout our churches of every denomination we see an increasing number of believers who are
realizing the fulfillment of Our Lord's promise: "Ye shall receive power after that the Holy Ghost is come upon you"
(Acts 1:8). In repsonse to their reborn faith, expectant hope
and revitalized love, He has bestowed upon them the gifts of
the Spirit in varying degree and kind, which they are using as

Paul adjured; unobtrusively, joyfully, to the glory of God and the edification of His Church (1 Cor. 14:12).

Our healing churches, filled again with the Holy Spirit, are vibrant with His power to heal and save. Purifying, cauterizing and empowering, He is indeed "Baptizing us with the Holy Ghost and with fire" (Luke 3:16).

What this renewal and resurgence of the Holy Spirit means, we can only guess. Could it possibly augur, I sometimes wonder, the fulfillment of Joel's prophecy? "And in the last days it shall be, God declares, that I will pour out my Spirit upon all flesh" (Acts 2:17 RSV).

Chapter 6

"according to your faith-"

Matt. 9:29

Recently a clergyman unfamiliar with the healing ministry invited me to address his ministerial association. "Please don't emphasize the place of faith in your talk," he said, "or you'll sound like a faith healer."

I had to refuse this invitation to speak, because I am convinced that faith is the crux of the whole matter. With faith we have everything; without it, nothing else matters. This is neither personal opinion nor hypothesis, but the teaching of Our Lord, who puts such enormous emphasis on faith as being necessary for salvation and healing. Again and again he says: "Thy faith hath saved thee" (Luke 18:42); "Thy faith hath made thee whole" (Luke 8:48). And He never ascribed failure to heal to anything *except* lack of faith. He Himself could not heal in an atmosphere of unbelief (Matt. 13:58); and when His disciples came to Him and said: "Why could not we heal the lunatic child?" Jesus answered swiftly and without equivocation: "Because of your unbelief" (Matt. 17:20).

And so it is today. I believe we must accept the necessity of an unreserved faith if we are to be healed. The fact that so many of us find it tortuously difficult to acquire, in no way obviates its necessity or mitigates its importance. The "healer's" belief is important, but it cannot substitute for the patient's. No one on earth can approximate the belief of Our Lord, yet *He* said: "According to *your* faith be it done to you." While it is true that the *entire* onus of faith should not be placed upon the patient, but should rest also with the Church, I think it an evasion of the truth to pretend that his faith or lack of it, is immaterial. The fact that it is actually of supreme importance, is impressed upon me every time I deal in any way with the sick. It was impressed upon me again just a few weeks ago.

My husband was out of town and it was close to midnight. I had just covered my typewriter and was on my way to bed, when the telephone rang. It was a woman from another city who had been corresponding with me about her condition—cancer. That afternoon her doctor had given her a completely negative prognosis, and on a sudden impulse she had flown to Pittsburgh. She was now calling me from a downtown hotel to ask me to see her.

I was tired and wanted to put her off until next morning, but her tone was so urgent, I got into my car and started off. All the way downtown I prayed that her faith would be strong. As I walked into the hotel room I breathed a sigh of relief as I felt her faith reach out, a viable thing, to meet mine. I knew instantly that something wonderful would happen that night, and it did. When I left her she was tranquil. She had received that gift of peace which only God can bestow.

She called next morning to say that for the first time in many weeks she had slept all night without a sedative. One grave external evidence of metastasis had already disappeared. It is far too soon to claim a healing, but her condition has dramatically improved.

I am well aware that some are healed who apparently lack faith; but for most of us, we must believe first. The longer I am associated with the healing ministry, the more convinced I become that the foremost requisite for healing lies in a simple faith in the promises of Jesus. "If thou canst believe, all things are possible," He says (Mark 9:23). "He that believeth on me, the works that I do shall he do also" (John 14:12). The ability to claim these promises depends on one single factor—the factor on which healing is contingent: namely our whole-hearted acceptance of Jesus as God.

It is to our everlasting shame and our own terrible deprivation that so many of us who profess to be Christians, have never *really* accepted the Lordship of Christ. If we had, we would unqualifiedly believe His words, simply because *He* spoke them; we would confidently claim His promises, simply because *He* made them. To whatever extent we disbelieve, to that exact extent do we reject Our Lord, and rob Christianity of its power—for although the *existence* of His healing grace is not dependent on our faith, its release *is*.

Christianity demands faith, not in an Ethic, but in a Person. As true spiritual healing means union with God, so for the Christian, access to His healing power must be by way of Jesus. If we want to be healed, we must stake everything we have on the supreme Reality, which is Jesus Christ, and His purpose for us, which is good. In the beginning, this will seem the greatest gamble you have ever taken. In the end you will find that it was actually not a gamble at all, but a sure thing.

In short, it is our unequivocal faith in Jesus, and our efforts to live in and by this faith, which comprise the basis and the essence of spiritual healing. It is just that simple—and for most of us, just that prodigiously difficult.

Because it *is* so difficult, we tend to take refuge in healing "techniques," which no matter how complex seem always easier than faith. These techniques are adjuncts to, but not substitutes for, faith. This is a gift of God which cannot be learned, only received. The tiniest grain—even the longing for it, is more effective than any known "method." Times without number we see demonstrated the eternal verity of His words:

"If ye have faith as a grain of mustard seed—nothing shall be impossible to you" (Matt. 17:20).

The experience of a man I talked with not long ago is a common one. "I tried to put the cart before the horse," he said. "I studied a number of books on prayer and healing, but while I learned *what* to pray, they couldn't teach me *how*. At the time I began attending healing services," he continued, "my faith was virtually non-existent. Nevertheless I *wanted* to believe, and God recognized my desire for faith in Him. As I continued to attend weekly services, my faith gradually increased until I felt closer to God than ever before. *Then* the techniques offered in these books became useful to me. Incidentally," he added, "I have been wonderfully healed of a throat tumor."

I have come to believe that a *whole* faith is actually the synthesis of two inseparable elements: the one, a fighting aggressive faith—an actual force which can move mountains and create miracles; and the other, a quiet trust and abiding confidence that God does all things well and never makes a mistake. Neither of these elements alone is sufficient, or can be said to comprise a total faith; for although the fighting faith is necessary to release the power of God, it is our *trust* in Him which permits our complete commitment, which in turn makes us receptive to His power.

There are still many, clergy and laity alike who, unfamiliar with the healing ministry, express apprehension that if a believer is *not* healed, he will be psychically damaged and lose his faith. Anyone even remotely associated with this ministry knows how unfounded is such a fear. No one who properly understands spiritual healing ever turns from God because he is not healed, for no one who turns to Him in faith remains unhealed spiritually. Further, no one who has experienced a healing of the spirit would exchange what he has received for a purely physical cure. But there are cases like that of a woman I know, of whom an uninformed observer might say:

"She wasn't healed, so she lost her faith." The truth is that she and other like supplicants, were never possessed of real faith in the first place.

The woman I speak of is suffering from a medically incurable disease. After the doctors had given her up, she frantically began to seek spiritual healing in much the same way as one would try a new drug. In spite of the fact that she appears to have an aggressive sort of faith, she has not been helped in any way. She has subsequently become bitter and resentful towards God. This in turn is blocking His healing power, so she is involved in a vicious circle from which she has been unable to extricate herself.

From the first, she has tried to *goad* God into healing her by the sheer force of her own faith; as if it were by virtue of *her* faith of itself, that she could be healed, instead of by the grace of God. She has never for even a moment, been able to commend herself to Him in trust. This predicament seems understandable, in a sense; for at first glance it seems difficult if not impossible, to reconcile the *expectant* faith we must hold for healing, with the simultaneous trust which permits us to say and mean it: "Though He slay me, yet will I put my trust in Him" (Job 13:14). This is the sort of paradox whose comprehension depends entirely on grace—a comprehension which cannot be intellectually rationalized, but must be spiritually discerned. This discernment can only come about through the Holy Spirit, whose power to instruct is no less wonderful than His power to heal.

There is no substitute for the fighting faith taught by Our Lord, which does vigorous battle against the forces of evil. But neither is there a substitute for the relaxed trust, which Our Lord also taught, and which, in the context of the healing ministry as in the Faith as a whole, is fundamental.

"Trust in the Lord with all thine heart" (Prov. 3:5), we are told—but Christian trust is never a supine or lethargic quality: it is the sort of supreme confidence which saved

Daniel in the lion's den; and can likewise protect us from the onslaughts of evil.

I think that neither of these elements of faith can be considered easy for most of us. Today's mores encourage us to intellectualize ourselves out of all faith; while the liberal Church, in an attempt to "keep up with the times," emphasizes *belief* rather than *faith*. Yet although we may believe with our intellects that an all-powerful Creator exists, there is no spiritual power in the belief of the mind; only in the faith of the heart and spirit, through which alone we can personally experience the greatness of God.

Several months ago I was asked to go to a hospital to pray for a child dying of nephritis. The hospital room was filled with relatives, all of whom ostensibly "believed" in God, but my heart sank as I felt the almost palpable aura of unbelief which surrounded the small patient. And then, glancing at the nurse, I saw a crucifix around her neck and asked if she were a Roman Catholic. She nodded—I could only say: "Thank God, then you believe in miracles. Please pray with me now that one will come to pass." It did. Within an hour the child's kidneys had begun to function; and within ten days she was home.

A total faith can take a long time to develop; and the one aspect of it may seem more difficult to you than the other. For me, probably because I came to my first real knowledge of God through the healing ministry, a "fighting" faith came easier than quiet trust. Having existed for so long by my mind in what I fondly thought was complete independence, it was extremely difficult to learn to live by faith in what I came to know was absolute dependence: to "lean not unto my own understanding"; to be wholly confident that He would direct my paths (Prov. 3:5, 6). You may find that the converse is true; but however it may be with you, if you possess either of these elements of faith, you may be sure that through the grace of the Holy Spirit, the other will follow as the night the day.

It is a remarkable fact that no matter how great or how small our faith may be at first, we do indeed grow from "faith to faith" (Rom. 1:17). It seems to progress according to our desire for God; and increase in relation to our effort to reach Him.

Recently a woman said: "I'm discouraged. I've been trying for years to acquire a really dynamic faith so that I can be healed. But this gift seems to have been withheld from me. I wonder why?"

God never withholds the gift of faith from those who seek Him with all their hearts. It occurred to me as she spoke, that her difficulty might perhaps lie in the words: "so that I can be healed."

"Knock and it shall be opened unto you," He said (Matt. 7:7). But He means the Kingdom, not only its fruits. "Seek and ye shall find" He said (Matt. 7:7). But He means Himself and not merely His gifts. If we want *Him* enough, I am completely certain that there is no one on earth who cannot receive Him; but if we want only the faith so that we may be physically healed, we are on the wrong track—for it is He, and not our faith, which makes us whole.

But regardless of the purity of our motives, many of us have discovered that the tenets of the Faith are more easily accepted by the mind than by the heart; and more readily received by the heart than known by the spirit. We cannot *wish* ourselves into faith, of this I am sure. But I am equally certain that we can be forged into it by the fire of the Holy Spirit, enkindled by our longing and ignited through our prayers.

When your faith is new, you may find the constant assaults upon it difficult to withstand. You may also find that intellectual pride may militate against your going all the way in your belief in the healing Christ.

As the mother of a mentally defective child put it: "Through the healing ministry I've come to believe that Mary can be healed. But not only is my faith being continually knocked down by the negative attitudes of my family and friends, but they make me feel downright stupid to believe in miracles in this day and age."

I have found that the best solution to this not uncommon situation, is to surround ourselves in so far as possible, with believers. Either join a prayer group or ask to be upheld in prayer; and try to attend a healing church where your faith will be activated and strengthened. As it grows you will find it a shield against the secular inference that faith and stupidity are synonomous.

I was once in the vanguard of those who so believe—but having so often seen the power of God released by simple faith, I now covet simplicity; and envy those so deeply blessed who need not devote precious time and effort towards becoming less complicated. I have learned for all time, that simplicity is not brainlessness; and that a childlike faith does not mean closing our eyes, but rather opening them wider. I have learned, too, that although God gave us our brains to use, there are times when we must lay aside our intellects—for it is only when our minds are stilled that the Holy Spirit can effectively work in us.

"But *how* can you still your mind?" asked a man who was gravely ill. "I trust in God, but because I know I may not be healed, my mind is proving a barrier to the expectant faith I know I should have."

Here I think a logical process of reasoning, based on statistics, can lead us to the point where the Holy Spirit can take over without hindrance.

Scores of healing clergymen unanimously conclude that 80% of all people who seek spiritual healing in their churches, regardless of how medically "hopeless" the disease from which they suffer, are either healed or sufficiently improved so that their life is prolonged far beyond medical expectancy. The remaining 20% receive no physical benefit, but experience extraordinary healings of the spirit.

One such case is that of a blind man who was once bitter against a God whom he felt had so afflicted him. This man still cannot see with his physical eyes, but he has received through the mercy of Christ so wonderful a spiritual insight, that no one, and least of all himself, could consider him sightless. Living and working and witnessing to the glory of God, many of us with whole bodies might well envy him his healing of the spirit. He seems not blinded by disease, but rather by the light of God, which illumines him and all who come in contact with him.

Through the healing ministry we have continual and dramatic evidence that if by faith we come closer to God, we *invariably* receive healing—and there are no exceptions. One of two things inevitably happens: either, as in the case of a once-paralysed man I know, your legs will again move; or equally wonderful, as in the case of a woman I know, you can live in peace with their lack of movement. As you progress into complete faith, your prayer for healing will subtly alter. You will pray that the healing Christ touch your life— but you no longer care *how*.

The other night an unbeliever challenged me. "You don't really *know* that God exists," he said. "You only *believe* that He does—and belief and knowledge are not the same thing."

Not too long ago I might have agreed with this statement, for I felt then that faith, not certitude, was all we could hope for on this earth. I see that I was wrong. As Christian hope is not a wish but complete assurance, so do I know now that Christian faith is not credulity, but certainty. And yet faith is not a static thing. It ebbs and rises and is almost impossible to sustain at a uniformly high level.

"I think I have seen every disease known, healed by the power of God," a clergyman told me recently; "yet each time before a healing service I have to struggle for faith."

I used to wonder why this was so, and why I, who was so sure, have had so often to battle for faith as if I had never possessed it. I am convinced now that it is because faith is of God and is peculiarly subject to the onslaught of the devil—or if you prefer, the forces of evil, by which the seeds of doubt are continually being sown.

As we perpetually need the help of God in overcoming evil, a deep and complete faith must involve that certainty of God's existence which enables us to share all our burdens with Him. Not the least of these is what we realize to be the inadequacy of our own faith. Perhaps it is those who know Him best who can most freely confess when it is necessary; "Lord, I believe; help thou mine unbelief" (Mark 9:24). He does not fail to honor either our desire or our plea. Even as we pray, we feel the faith we thought we lacked, surge up within us.

Faith, love and repentance are the cornerstones of the healing ministry and they are so inextricably part of one another and of healing, that it is difficult if not impossible to separate them. Often Our Lord did not seem to try, but appeared to consider them indivisible. "Her sins, which are many, are *forgiven*; for she *loved* much," He said; and then He quickly added: "Thy sins are forgiven; thy *faith* hath saved thee" (Luke 7:47-50).

In these words lie all we need to know of spiritual healing —but it is faith which is the matrix. "For whatsoever is born of God overcometh the world: and this is the victory that overcometh the world, even our faith" (1 John 5:4). Christ dwell in our hearts by faith (Eph. 3:17); through faith in His Name are we made whole (Acts 3:16); and by faith in Him as the Son of God are we saved (Acts 16:31).

"Fear not, only believe," He said. Our prayers for faith should be unceasing, for we can never have enough. Again and again He makes this unequivocally clear. "Did I not tell you that if you would believe, you would see the glory of God?" (John 11:40) There is no other way.

Chapter 7

"restore thou those who are penitent"

BCP - Gen. Con.

The struggle for faith is unremitting, for without it we cannot receive Him: but even our faith is "vain if we are yet in our sins (1 Cor. 15:17).

Our acknowledgement of sin, our penitence and God's forgiveness are the warp and woof of the Christian Faith—the meaning and the purpose of the Redemption.

"Except ye repent," Our Lord said, "ye shall all likewise perish" (Luke 13:3). And unless our souls are cleansed by His absolving grace, we can know neither Him nor His healing power.

At first glance repentance would seem the easiest of the requisites of the Faith to fulfil, but for me it has not proved so. It has often seemed incredibly difficult to make a wholly honest act of contrition. The problem of differentiating between real penitence and a desire to realize God's benefits has been a very real one for me and I have good reason to suspect, for many.

Two questions continually assailed me: Was I sorry merely because my sins were blocking me from God's power; or was I sorry because they had hurt Christ? Was I recognizing with my intellect alone, an error of omission or word or thought or deed, for which I knew I *should* be sorry; or was I truly seeking forgiveness of sin which I acknowledged with my heart as well as with my mind? It was when I fully realized that not *much* but *everything* depended on the answers to these questions, that I adopted the practice of invariably preceding my prayer for forgiveness by a heartfelt prayer that I might *honestly* repent.

This was when I learned to pray, first with my lips, and finally with my heart: "Against thee, thee only have I sinned" (Psalm 51:4).

This was when I learned that in response, a merciful God reaches down into the little hells we create for ourselves; and "making clean our hearts within us" (BCP, p. 31) transforms them by His touch.

This was when I learned that penitence is the result of His grace and not our effort.

I have been the grateful recipient of this grace times without number, and I have seen it frequently bestowed on the uncertain and confused.

Take for example, the case of a woman who came to me a few months ago, wondering why she had not received healing.

"I believe thoroughly that Christ heals," she said; "and I've been attending healing services for a year, but with no apparent benefit." She went on to explain that for several years before she had been engaged in an extra-marital affair. "But that was all over a year ago," she said, "and I have asked God's forgiveness." Then anxiously she added: "You *do* think He has forgiven me, don't you?"

Before I had time to reply, she inadvertently supplied a clue to the problem. "Of course no one was hurt," she commented thoughtfully. "The affair just burned itself out, and my husband was never the wiser." The question then was not the forgiveness of God, which is never in doubt, but the sincerity of her contrition.

I sensed in her situation a dilemma which confronts many of us from time to time, whether our sin happens to be adultery or an explosive temper; selfishness or gossip; irritability or resentment. Had she confessed because she was genuinely sorry and longed to reestablish her relationship with God; or had she made an unintentionally empty gesture, because she now needed His healing power?

Was she like the man I had seen the week before who had been involved in a shady business deal and was now enjoying its fruits. "I've repented," he had said, "and I can't understand why there still seems to be a barrier between me and God." Yet in the next breath he had said in justification of his act: "I simply had to have the money." When I asked him if he would repeat the same offence if the time should come again when he "had" to have the money, he could not answer.

Had this woman, too, subconsciously harbored the thought that once having achieved her desire—once having accomplished what she wanted to do, she would then, and only then, seek forgiveness? Given the same opportunity, would she do the same thing again?

It was a long time before she could give an honest answer to these questions; but through prayer and grace she has come at last to a state of sincere penitence. The impasse to Him at last removed, her health, both spiritual and physical, has been restored. Today she is a transformed person.

On the other side of the coin, and as spiritually unrewarding as a reserved confession, is the attitude of the unquestionably remorseful, who say again and again: "I have committed so terrible a sin that I know God can't possibly forgive it." Frequently this attitude is the result of our unwitting and perverted pride, which assumes that *our* sin is greater than anyone's else. It is actually a denial on our parts, of His promise and power to forgive. It is placing a human limitation on His compassion, which is limitless. In this connection I sometimes think of Judas, and dare to wonder if perhaps his most monstrous sin was not his betrayal of Jesus, but his lack of faith that Our Lord could and would forgive him.

Alcoholics Anonymous has discovered in treating alcoholics,

that the primary step in the rehabilitation of the drinker, must be his free acknowledgement that he is an alcoholic; and so it seems to me it is with sin. We are deprived of God's forgiveness until we admit to ourselves that we sin—and cease to slough off whatever we do or think as "human shortcomings"—so trivial as to be unworthy of repentance, and so trifling as not to warrant absolution. It is by our increasing discernment of sin, that our spirits are opened to His absolving grace. It is when we draw near to His healing light, that the burden of our sins does indeed become intolerable. It is when we finally come to acknowledge our parts in His Crucifixion, that we begin to fully realize our legacy in His Resurrection.

"But," someone protested recently, "doesn't all this preoccupation with sin encourage morbid introspection?"

This question rang a familiar bell, for it had been mine for so many years, when the Church's emphasis on sin had seemed to me, who was then outside it, unhealthy, unrealistic and antediluvian. Only recently have I begun to know the full enormity of my error. My answer today to such a question can only be an unequivocal and emphatic NO.

Working in the healing ministry, it has been my observation that those who are not concerned with their own sins are inclined to be inordinately concerned with the sins of others; and while I readily concede that for me, at least, self-examination is always dismaying, often frightening and frequently extremely painful, it is never morbid.

I believe that for the Christian, a continuous awareness of how far short we come of Him, can never result in a neurosis; for I have learned that in direct proportion to our consciousness of sin, God's forgiveness pours over and into us, cleansing, purifying and strengthening us in direct relation to our penitence. The greater our contrition, the more marvellously abundant is His stream of absolving grace.

"Heal my soul, for I have sinned against thee" (Psalm 41:4). Through His grace our plea is answered. By this grace, we are drawn continually closer to Him. In this grace I have found, as have countless thousands before me, healing which defies description.

Many of us are well aware of our easily identifiable sins of the flesh; but most of us tend to overlook or underestimate the destructive capacity of those sins of the spirit of which we are all guilty to a greater or lesser extent. Our physical health as well as our spiritual lives may depend upon our recognition of these for what they are; for "If we say that we have no sin, we deceive ourselves" (1 John 1:8).

A year ago a woman to whom the healing ministry was new, spoke to me concerning her medically termed "irreversible" impairment of vision, which had been accompanied by frequent and incapacitating headaches.

"I can't understand why I haven't been healed," she said. "I work for, and give to the Church, and I'm certainly not guilty of any of the so-called spiritual sins." Yet within five minutes I heard her vouchsafe that "all Roman Catholics are so bigoted I can't stand the sight of any of them"; "all Jews are shysters"; and "my son-in-law is a perpetual headache to me."

This woman lived in a predominantly Roman Catholic neighborhood, a mile from her daughter and son-in-law, and her husband worked for a Jewish concern. She was literally drowning in a sea of her own hostility. When this was pointed out, she began to make a sincere effort to change her attitudes. God honors our slightest impulse towards Him, and He has honored hers. She told me recently that she had not suffered a headache in over three months; and to her doctor's amazement, her vision has dramatically improved.

"If we confess our sins, He is faithful and just to forgive us" (1 John 1:9). But first we must recognize these sins in ourselves; and this often requires considerable soul-searching —and always the help of the Holy Spirit, Who convinces us of sin as surely as He comforts (Heb. 7:25).

Take the case of a devout Christian with a good understanding of the healing ministry and an unshakable faith in the healing Christ. She had attended healing services for months without any apparent physical improvement in her arthritic condition, which regardless of medical treatment and prayer had continued to grow progressively worse.

"I felt in myself a definite impediment to God's healing power," she said, "but examine myself as I might, I couldn't unearth the trouble. And then one day as I prayed, I asked the Holy Spirit to guide me into a knowledge of my sin. That same night I saw in the paper the name of a woman I had quarrelled with years before, over an injustice I felt she had done me. Suddenly I knew that this was it. I immediately prayed forgiveness for my own sin in the matter, and at once I sensed the lifting of a great burden. Next time I received the laying on of hands, I prayed for her as I did for myself. God's power surged through me at that moment. I am now completely healed."

In obedience to His Command to preach repentance and the remission of sins in His Name (Luke 24:27), every branch of the Church offers some means of confession within the context of its service. In addition to the Corporate Confession of all Protestant churches, the Episcopal Church offers the private sacramental Confession, which differs from the obligatory Roman Catholic Sacrament in that "all *can*, but none *must*."

To many Protestants, including Episcopalians, the idea of the sacramental Confession is abhorrent; but it is interesting to note that Dr. John Bonnell, pastor of the Fifth Avenue Presbyterian Church, extols its benefits, pointing out that the great leaders of the Reformation such as Luther, Calvin and Knox, all advocated its use.

Perhaps in ruthlessly discarding the Sacrament of Penance as a repugnant Romish custom, we have thrown out the baby with the bath water; for all over the nation I have observed a growing awareness of the need for a more specific act of contrition than the General Confession allows. This need is being met in many churches by informal confession in the pastor's study—and in the Episcopal Church by an increased use by its members, of the sacramental Confession.

But it is the forgiveness of God which heals our souls—not the method by which it is received, which is of importance only to the penitent. His saving grace is available to all of us, at all times, wherever we may be. Yet as His Presence is intensified in Holy Communion; as it is uniquely abundant in the Healing Church, so, for many of us, is His redemptive power curiously concentrated in the Sacrament of Penance. By no other means are we able to feel so marvellously empty of sin, however temporary the respite; and so filled again with the Holy Spirit.

But I believe in the sacramental Confession not only because of what it does for me, but because of what I have so often seen it do for others.

Take for example a man who had received the laying on of hands several times, but now felt a need for Unction. When he discovered that special preparation was necessary to receive this specific healing Sacrament—in this case the priest in charge required a sacramental Confession—the man hesitated. Although an Episcopalian he had never availed himself of the Sacrament of Penance and was not at all sure that he wanted to begin now. After lengthy consideration, he finally went ahead. "I've never felt so wonderful," he said afterwards, "or so completely healed. My only regret is that for so many years I have missed out because of prejudice."

Or take the woman who at the age of fifty, made her first such Confession under similar circumstances, and later said to me: "I had sought God's healing power for three years. Until that day, I had not received it. It was my pride which had kept me from accepting this Sacrament before." It may well have been this pride which had constituted a barrier to His healing power. I am sure that no one should be urged to make an auricular Confession if he is opposed; but I am equally sure that it is often through making such a Confession, which is never easy, at least for me, that the last, destructive vestige of spiritual pride is removed—and healing subsequently occurs.

Psychoanalysis and religion are in accord on two points: the therapeutic effect of the confessional (although they differ on the correct posture to assume), and the danger of carrying a burden of unrelieved guilt. But while the psychoanalyst uncovers guilt, he cannot absolve it—and only in absolution lies complete healing.

This is not to say that no one needs psychiatric treatment—but only that we should not confuse the comparatively few who are mentally unbalanced and need a psychiatrist, with the spiritually unbalanced which includes most of us, who need to confess continually on our knees that we may remain permanently off our backs.

The only danger in the Christian's concern with sin, lies in the possibility that he cannot wholly accept the forgiveness of God. It is true that Our Lord cautions us that "If ye forgive not men their trespasses neither will your Father forgive your trespasses" (Matt. 6:15); and time after time we see this truth demonstrated in the healing ministry. A woman is at last able to forgive her husband's infidelity, and God's saving power flows unrestricted through her disease-ridden body, bringing healing in its wake. A man, deaf for twenty years, finally forgives the malice of his son, and through the redeeming power of God, his hearing is restored. And yet there are times when it seems more difficult to *receive* forgiveness than to *give* it. These are the times when for many of us, the sacramental Confession provides the contact and the channel through which this infinitely wonderful grace can ultimately be received.

Charles Morrison has said that "The Christian Church is the only society in the world which is based on the single qualification that the candidate shall be unworthy of membership."

Apropos of this, a man announced the other night, that

after twenty-five years of membership in the Church, he was leaving it. "I just can't stand the 'crawling' to God that the Church demands," he said. "I don't believe we're utterly depraved, and I don't think I or anyone else is 'unworthy.' We are the sons of God, and he evidently thought us 'worthy' enough to die for."

In a sense this is true. I would thoroughly agree that we are not depraved, but I could not deny that we are sinful. I must believe that we are fallen, but I know that we can be raised, for God is continually lifting us up to a state better than we are. The wonderful and religiously unique thing about the Incarnation, is that Jesus, as God, lived among men as fully Man. He knows that we have sorrows to endure as well as sins to expiate. We "all have sinned and come short" (Rom. 3:23); yet as our sins continue to crucify Christ, so does our atonement for them, to some small degree, justify His Sacrifice. In His death for us, He has bestowed upon us an inalienable dignity—a stature which we should never undervalue. But our dignity is not impaired by our dependence on Him; nor our stature decreased by our continuing need for His saving grace. We can never, of ourselves, be worthy, yet His grace can make us so.

Time and time again, the first instinctive cry of those who have known His healing power is: "Lord, I am not worthy"; and my own heart continually echoes it. It is a cry involuntarily wrested from our souls, as for a fleeting instant we stand in the Presence of His complete holiness.

If faith, love and repentance are the keys to healing, the tenuous strand on which they hang is humility. If this breaks, the keys are lost, and so are we.

Recently I talked with a woman who had read widely on spiritual healing. She was saying all the right words, but underlying them I sensed what seemed to me an almost terrifying lack of humility—an attitude of judgment of God.

She attended a healing service the following day, and there

sat beside her a woman scheduled to have her leg amputated, who said: "I came here today not to ask for healing, but only to thank God for all He has done for me; and to pray that He will stand beside me in the operating room." This woman was miraculously healed that day, and no amputation was necessary. My friend's reaction was; "I *know* that I had more faith than she did. God should have healed *me* instead."

It has been my experience that without humility it is hopeless to seek healing. God will respond to even the faintest stirring of contrition in our hearts; He will honor even our *striving* for faith; He will bless even our *desire* to love; but He will not tolerate in us a lack of humility. And so far as I know, humility is something which cannot be taught. The proud do not know they lack it; and the humble do not know they possess it. This is one area in which I think each of us must pray continuously for ourselves; for to pray for the humility of others is in itself an act of arrogance.

Sin separates us from God, which is why "the wages of sin is death" (Rom. 6:23); but Our Lord makes clear that the direct route back to Him and to life, is via the road of repentance. No sin, however flagrant, can close this road—only the self-erected barricade of our own impenitence.

Beseeching the guidance of the Holy Spirit, we fall to our knees, and with hearts and minds and voices pray: "Search me, O God, and know my heart; try me and know my thoughts: and see if there be any wicked way in me" (Psalm 139:23, 24).

In merciful and swift response, He proffers us the healing grace of His absolution.

Chapter 8

redemptive suffering

Just as my belief that God does not will disease is unshakable, so is my conviction that although saints most assuredly can be sick, saintliness and sickness are by no means synonomous.

Much contact with the sick over the past several years has demonstrated to me beyond any doubt that generally speaking, illness does not tend to sanctify the sufferer, but quite the reverse. I have seen that physical suffering is not inclined to elevate the spirit, but in the majority of cases degrades its victims to a purely animalistic level where the only reality is pain, and the only desire its alleviation.

Some, to be sure, endure pain with fortitude, but it is a fortitude which more often derives from the Stoic philosophy than the love of God; and most exhibit bitterness or querulousness, resentment or peevishness, commensurate with the gravity of the affliction or the discomfort it induces. A nagging headache or a bad cold tends to ruin the best of dispositions; and if you are like most of us, Christian or not, and have ever suffered even a severe toothache, your chief interest at the time was probably in reaching the dentist—not the Kingdom. It is not difficult to understand then, how someone suffering the agony of cancer is more apt to focus his attention on his next injection of demarol than on God.

And yet suffering *can* be truly redemptive. When this occurs, which in my experience is less often than physical healing and perhaps even more impressive to witness, I confess myself completely awed by the wonder of it.

I know a young woman thirty years of age, for example, who has experienced a profound spiritual rebirth, but whose entire body is invaded by cancer. She lies flat on her back, able to move only one arm and leg, and in continuous and intense pain. Cheerful and strangely happy, she utters no word of complaint, for pain has no dominion over her.

Receiving regularly the healing Sacraments of the Church, her faith and the love of God shine in her serene eyes. Every breath she draws seems drawn to His glory, her suffering consecrated and her spirit sanctified by Him. The word "death" is not in her vocabulary, for she is truly alive in Jesus Christ—an awesome example of His power to convert the evil of disease to a holy purpose.

Her case and others like it, seem to me to demonstrate the vast and vital difference between hopeless resignation to an unhappy fate, and that expectant faith which in His Name gives us the victory over pain and disease and death; a victory He has already won for us, and which, by His grace, we can all claim.

Resignation, as fortitude, is not necessarily a Christian virtue; for as the unbeliever can endure, so can he passively "accept."

If we piously resign ourselves to sickness, congratulating ourselves on our meek surrender to what we expediently term "God's will," we are not offering Him our courage, but our defeat. We are not demonstrating our nobility but our lack of discernment; for resignation implies an attitude of vanquishment, not victory. It is quite different from that wholehearted Christian acceptance (which actually is more *receiving* than *accepting*) in which there is a sort of triumph born of the knowledge that we are denied not for the sake of denial, but for His sake; that we are martyred not for the sake of martyrdom, but for Him.

To be able with peace and joy to offer our suffering to God, to be enabled by His power to transmute involuntary affliction into *voluntary* sacrifice and thus to be crucified with Christ (Gal. 2:20), may well be the highest privilege we know. It is one exercised by only a few.

Not very long ago I could not at all comprehend the ascetic practice of mortification of the body. While I have not changed my belief that self-inflicted suffering is inconsistent with God's will and therefore has no place in the Christian Faith, I nevertheless can now understand, through my witness of redemptive suffering, the impulse to sacrifice which prompted it.

A few months ago I prayed with a woman whose desperate illness had been miraculously transformed from the meaningless horror it had once been, to a glorious instrument of redemption. Afterwards, a friend of the patient was to say to me: "I don't know how she can keep her faith. How can people who suffer as she does believe that God really cares about any of us?"

They believe because they see in the Crucifixion the answer to this question for all time, for all people. They know that Jesus' Heart as well as His Body was broken for us on the Cross. They know that they do not bear their pain alone; that He suffers *with* us today as surely as He suffered *for* us twenty centuries ago. And above all, they know that "the sufferings of this present time are not worthy to be compared to the glory which shall be revealed" (Rom. 8:18), for fragmentary glimmers of this glory is a part of all redemptive suffering.

Two years ago I knew a little girl of seven who during the last year of her life glimpsed more than a little of it, and shared her knowledge with me as she did with all who knew her.

I first met Kristin Franz in April, 1959, during a healing

mission at St. Matthew's Episcopal Church in Kenosha, Wisconsin.

On the first two morning of the Mission, I had seen her father carry the extraordinarily pretty little red-haired girl to the altar rail to receive the laying on of hands. On the third day I found out who she was when her parents asked for a consultation with me.

An attractive and highly intelligent couple, they explained that Krissie, always an active and robust child, had been struck down six months before by sarcoma of the bone.

The medical prognosis was completely negative: rapid metastasis, steadily increasing pain, and within months, an agonizing death.

Amputation of the affected leg had been considered, and the idea rejected. Such a procedure offered at best only a short prolongation of pain-racked life, to which would be added the emotional distress of maiming.

Already hospitalized a number of times, the child had by now received the maximal amount of X-ray treatment and a new drug had been experimentally used in a desperate and apparently futile attempt to halt the disease.

Spiritual healing had only recently come to the attention of the parents, who had brought Krissie to Kenosha at the suggestion of an Episcopal clergyman in Madison where she had been hospitalized.

I found them devout and hopeful, with unusual spiritual insight into the ministry of healing for those so recently acquainted with it. This Mission was their first experience with the ministry in action, and their faith was strong that Christ in His mercy would lay His healing Hand upon their little girl. During the three days they had been in Kenosha, Krissie had already rather remarkably responded.

When, after our talk, they brought her into me for special prayer, she walked into the room of her own accord, only a slight limp being discernible. I found her outgoing and vivacious, far more absorbed with the new bicycle she was sure she was soon going to be able to ride, "because Jesus is healing me," than with her sore leg, which she understood to have been "broken."

I prayed for her that day with complete confidence, claiming her healing in the Name of Jesus Christ.

Immediately after the laying on of hands, the Franz family left to take the long drive home. "Along the way," Mrs. Franz wrote me a month later, "I detected an odor of something burning—or intense heat—and I asked my husband if something could be on fire. We found nothing wrong, and suddenly Krissie commented that she was very warm and wanted to take off her sweater. Although both her father and I wore coats, she rode all the way home in a short-sleeved cotton dress without even a sweater. She had been very pale, but now I noticed that her cheeks were flushed, and I wondered if she had fever. And then I remembered your description of the phenomenon of intense heat which is often associated with the healing power. Krissie's pallor has not returned, and not only has her color improved, but her appetite and her whole personality. She suddenly became, and has remained, happy contented and sweet, and much less demanding than she had been for many weeks. That first afternoon home she walked around furniture with no one supporting her, for twenty-six consecutive steps."

There was no doubt of Krissie's dramatic improvement the day after they returned from the Mission. She not only drove with her parents to the local drugstore, but got out with them and edged her way along the counters admiring the displays.

The local doctor, a Dutch refugee, happened to be in the store at the time, and after looking at the child, questioned Mr. Franz closely concerning the accuracy of the diagnosis of sarcoma. He commented that he had seen many such cases in Holland where it is less rare than here, and had never known an instance where the patient recovered even a brief measure of health such as was now apparent to him in Kristin. "This is nothing short of miraculous!" he exclaimed.

Her strength and general sense of well-being increased at an extremely rapid rate, and she accepted without question the fact that God had healed her.

When she returned to the hospital over a month later for her check-up, the X-rays showed decided improvement, and while there was still evidence of the growth, it had markedly regressed.

The doctors on the hospital staff were surprised and delighted. One, on being told of the healing prayer being offered for Krissie and of how she had received the healing Sacraments of the Church, urged the Franzes to continue this course of spiritual therapy as he felt that this had been a significant factor in her improvement—an improvement which in his opinion could not be attributed to the medical treatment rendered her.

Other attending physicians reminded the parents that never in medical history had there been recorded a cure of this disease, and regardless of the present indications, warned them of what they felt was the inevitability of the child's death. To this, the Franzes replied: "We faced Krissie's death before, when we were without hope. We believe now with all our hearts that she will live—but we also know that whatever happens, God will not withhold His grace from us or from her."

Kristin was dismissed from the hospital with the word that the diseased bone was now sufficiently restored to warrant normal play activity. The family thanked God, and went home rejoicing.

For six weeks the child led the active and happy life of any other seven-year-old—and then one night she awoke screaming with the pain in her leg.

Hospitalized again for a final course of the powerful drug

therapy, she was sent home ten days later, weak, withdrawn, and much of the time in pain.

At this point her parents called me to ask my opinion of the advisability of taking Kristin to St. Stephen's Episcopal Church in Philadelphia, noted for its powerful healing ministry under the leadership of the Rev. Alfred Price. "We all feel the need of the spiritual support of people who believe in the healing Christ," Mrs. Franz said; "and we want to protect Krissie from the complete negativism of our town. We feel that if she is surrounded with the extraordinary love and marvellous faith which seem to radiate from those in the healing ministry, she will respond as she did at Kenosha."

It was clearly obvious that every bit of spiritual power which could be marshalled through positive prayer and the healing Church was necessary to battle what was a very real and terrible adversary. As the child was anxious to make the trip and her doctors were agreeable, I did not discourage the pilgrimage.

Krissie stood the plane trip remarkably well, and was quiet and unusually thoughtful throughout the service. Carried back to her pew after receiving the laying on of hands, the parents were again aware of the strong burning odor of intense heat they had noted after leaving Kenosha.

And as before, there was a marked improvement in the child's condition, but this time the respite was short-lived. On July 1 she entered the hospital for what was to prove her final check-up. Her condition was found to be considerably worse, and she was sent home to die.

The parents never lost hope, nor she her confidence, that God was healing her. The faith of the whole family increased rather than diminished during the ordeal of pain-filled days and nights that followed. Their spiritual growth was in itself a miracle—impressive evidence of the healing Christ at work. The love of God undergirded their every task, and prayer became a way of life. It was offered, in shifts, twenty-four hours a day, with Krissie often praying with them. As the pain increased and became impervious to drugs, it was only prayer that could relieve the little patient. When the relief came, tears of joy would stream down her face, as she cried: "See, Mommie, Jesus heard our prayers and has made the pain stop!"

From the beginning, Kristin had proved enormously receptive to God's power. Many prayer groups all over the country were offering prayer for her, and whenever there was a concerted effort of prayer, dramatic improvement in her condition was noted, but it seemed impossible to sustain. This temporary improvement was not imagination or wishful thinking based on prior knowledge that prayer was being offered at a given time. Again and again, for example, I fasted and prayed and received the laying on of hands for her—and on several occasions asked that Holy Communion be offered at my Church with Special Intention for her—most often without the knowledge of the Franzes. It was almost uncanny how invariably would come word from them that at the exact time these things were done, Krissie had taken a turn for the better: the pain had suddenly ceased; or she had suddenly said she was hungry when she had refused food for days; or she had begun to play games again when she hadn't lifted her head off the pillow for days before.

On one occasion when she was screaming in agony which drugs could not mitigate, her mother went into another room and called long distance to request a clergyman for prayer over the telephone. When she returned to Krissie's room the bed was empty. The little girl who had been unable to move herself for weeks, and a few moments before had been hysterical with pain, was found in another room, smiling and standing before the mirror brushing her hair.

There was no healing Church of any kind in the Franzes' town, and denominational barriers were disregarded as for over three months an Episcopal priest travelled a hundred miles round trip every Friday to anoint the small patient and offer Holy Communion to the family, not Episcopalians, at an improvised altar in Krissie's room.

For several days after each such Sacramental healing service, her condition seemed improved. She was aware of this and soon began to ask her parents to pray when ever she felt the pain beginning. It became an everyday occurrence to hear her call out to whoever was home at the moment, "Will you please come and pray?"

The spiritual change in Krissie was by now almost startlingly apparent. During her long and torturous illness she had naturally enough become extremely spoiled and demanding, while the pain had made her continually cross and irritable. But now she had become extraordinarily solicitous about her parents, deeply concerned with over-tiring them, their lack of sleep and their worry over her discomfort. She would insist that they lie down at night and try to sleep. On numerous occasions she would urge them to go into the garden for a while, assuring them that she would be all right without them because: "I know Jesus is here. I can feel His Hand on my head."

Over and over again she told them how much she loved them. There was no hint of disillusionment or disappointment, and no vestige of rebellion that she was not yet healed. There never is in the true believer, and least of all in a child, whose spiritual understanding seems innate. Krissie grew painlessly and imperceptibly into the knowledge that Our Lord would heal her in His own way and in His own time.

She no longer complained about her pain or incapacitation. "I'm just *sure* I'll be able to ride my bike in the autumn," she said more than once. "Do you know why I'm so sure? Because I'm just *learning* how to pray after all this time."

Whatever she did now, she did for the pleasure of others, coloring pictures for her friends and trying to make patterns of the pot holders she wove, particularly pretty. (Among my most treasured possessions is one she wove for me after her eyesight had begun to fail. The colors may not be orthodox, but to me they are the prettiest I have ever seen.)

Her love of beauty increased day by day. Each flower that summer seemed to her a new miracle from God; and all day long she would wait for the sunset, and glory in its splendor which bathed the confines of her small world.

As her physical condition grew more appalling, she seemed correspondingly filled with peace and that overwhelming love which comes only from God.

She spoke more and more of love in those last days. "I love *everybody*," she'd say. "I mean *really* love them," and she would name names of everyone she had ever known; then, turning to her parents, say: "Of course I love you two the most, except for Jesus. You don't mind if I love Him just a *little* more, do you?" And often she would reflect: "You know, I feel so sorry for lots of people because I know Him so well, and they don't."

A short while before she died in October, she seemed suddenly and horrifiedly aware of her pitiful, distorted body. Strangely withdrawn from her parents, she held up her little arms and called over and over again, "I want Jesus—I want Jesus." Her parents knelt beside her then, and prayed that she would be released to Him. Their hands on her head, they committed to Him her spirit. She relaxed and breathed quietly for about ten minutes, and gently He took her to Himself, where safe in His healing arms, she knew the end of pain.

The priest who had ministered to Krissie, said that he felt she had attained sainthood some three weeks before she died.

Those of us who knew her—who suffered over her horrifying physical deterioration, could at the same time only marvel at how her pain was used for the glory of God. Marvel, and know a curious envy that she knew the Christ as could none of us.

No one can accurately estimate the number of lives influenced and yet to be touched, by this little girl whose illness spanned one entire year of her short life. To those of us who knew her, our lives will never again be quite the same.

An interdenominational hospital chapel is being built as a memorial to her—and in the planning and the furnishing, the local churches have united in a joint effort for the first time in the town's history. Many will kneel in this chapel in the years to come, built in a very real sense by Kristin Franz, that His Name might be glorified.

St. Mary's Mission was born around the kitchen table in the Franzes' home, where throughout the winter following Krissie's death, classes of instruction, Sunday school and services of worship were conducted by the clergyman who had brought the Church to the little girl during her illness. In the spring her brothers and parents were among those confirmed in the Episcopal Church. Having claimed the victory by the grace of the Holy Spirit, the Franzes are living their lives to the Glory of God; magnificent witnesses to, and for, the healing Christ.

After Krissie's death people were to say to me: "It's awfully sad, of course, but it was God's will. And just think how her parents have grown spiritually, and the inspiration she was to all their friends and neighbors!"

My answer was simple: the God I worship does not unspeakably torture a small child that her parents may know salvation or her friends and neighbors be "inspired." The God I love did not *will* her hideous sickness, but He used it. He did not *will* her agonizing death, but He sanctified her spirit in an extraordinary and wonderful way—and all of us who came within her sphere received a vicarious benediction.

"And a little child shall lead them" (Isa. 11:6). She has indeed.

Chapter 9

the presence

Not long ago a friend told me in consternation that she had never felt the Presence of God. She asked for any suggestions I could make, and then she said: "But perhaps everyone isn't meant to know it, and perhaps I never shall. What do you think?"

I believe implicitly that anyone who wants Him enough can know His Presence. On the basis of my own experience, I am convinced that the answer lies in the word "want," for I have come to believe that it is the extent of our *desire* for God, even more than the degree of our need, which brings us to Him, and Him to us.

"Behold, I stand at the door and knock: if any man hear my voice, and open the door, I will come in to him" (Rev. 3:20). We all know agnostics or atheists who have suffered and withstood, without the acknowledged help of God, their afflictions. Their need of God may have seemed great, but only their longing for Him could enable them to hear His voice and open the door so that He might enter their hearts.

Just as in healing it is when we want God more than our physical cure, that we are most likely to receive bodily healing, so it is when a quiet awareness of Him seems more important to us than a demonstration of His power, that we are most assured of knowing His Presence. To believe that He means any of us to remain perpetually unaware of Him is as unthinkable as to assume that He wishes us to deny His existence. I can only concur with Mother Julian, who wrote in the fourteenth century: "He willeth that we believe that we see Him continually—and in this belief He maketh us evermore to gain grace. For He will be sought and He will be seen."

As the existence of God does not depend upon our acknowledgement of Him, so the actuality of His Presence does not depend upon our recognition of it. Wherever we are and under all circumstances, each of us is continually surrounded by Him whether or not we are actively aware of it. Nevertheless, it is an indisputable fact that His love and healing power become available to us in direct accordance with our *conscious* identity with Him and our confession of His reality as the living God.

To cultivate our awareness so that we may *know* when we stand in His Presence, takes for many of us considerable time and practice. As there is more than one road to faith; as there is more than one way to pray, so is there more than one way of practicing the Presence of God. I can only tell you of how it has been with me.

It was a long time after I had intellectually accepted the premise that God continually surrounds and pervades each one of us, that I actually knew His Presence and recognized it as such.

It began one night as I prayed during my husband's illness.

For the first few days after his return home from the hospital, I was able to pray fairly confidently; but it soon became obvious that I wasn't as confident as I had thought. As the days went by and the nervous strain accumulated, my prayers gradually deteriorated into an incessant, and even then I realized powerless, repetition of, "Please God heal him—Please God heal him"—and not much else. Then one night I was too tired to pray at all except, "Lord have mercy. I believe, help thou mine unbelief."

Suddenly the profound longing for my husband's physical healing was replaced by what I can only describe as an overwhelming spiritual thirst. Simultaneously there washed over me a feeling, not at all of resignation, but of indescribable peace. At that moment there was a sudden instantaneous flash of awareness which went as quickly as it had come—so quickly, indeed, that time-wise, the experience might well have been attributed to wishful thinking or an over-active imagination. Yet the impact was so tremendous and so lasting, that were I never to have had that experience again, I think I could not for the remainder of my life, have denied that it actually happened.

Many months went by before a repetition of this experience, and it was during these months that, for the first time, I began to meditate as well as pray; to become absolutely still and abide in the love of God, confident that He was well aware of the situations in which by prayer alone, I had sought to elicit His response.

This was the period in which I learned to contemplate God in all of His majesty and all of His mercy; to meditate each day on some of His words.

"He that loseth his life for my sake, shall find it" (Matt. 10:39).

"He that taketh not his cross, and followeth after me, is not worthy of me (Matt. 10:38).

"Out of his heart shall flow rivers of living water" (John 7:38).

"If any one thirst, let him come to me and drink" (John 7:37).

"I am the way, the truth and the life" (John 14:6).

This was the period in which the words: "Be still and know that I am God," became more than a phrase from the 46th Psalm. They became fact.

"Silence is the element in which great things fashion themselves," said Carlyle. It was in this silence that I learned to listen to God—and in the listening, at last to hear Him.

There are some who tend to use meditative prayer almost exclusively; but for most people, as for me, a combination of meditation and prayer have proved the best answer—the most effective means of realizing the Presence. It is as if through prayer we reach out to touch the Hem of the Garment; while by meditation we are enveloped in it. The reaching out is as vital as the enfoldment: each is dependent on the other.

This is part, although only a part, of the practice of the Presence, by which means that initial flash of awareness may be repeated and gradually sustained over longer periods of time.

I soon learned that the practice of the Presence could not be confined to an hour or so a day of prayer and meditation, but is actually a twenty-four-hour-a-day proposition. It means offering yourself to God when you get up in the morning, and giving yourself to Him when you go to sleep at night, with His Name in your heart and on your lips; and in your mind, affirmations of His Being: "I am the Lord thy God." "I am the Lord that healeth thee." "I will be unto thee an everlasting light." "The Lord is my strength and my shield." "And ye shall seek me and find me." Throughout the night He will thus be present in your subconscious, to which He has easy and unimpeded access.

It means throughout the day an acknowledgement, if not yet a *sense*, of His continued Presence, by the frequent saying of little prayers of praise and thanksgiving, however short, as you make the beds or ride to the office. Even a silent repetition of the Name of Jesus will suffice—"A Name which is above every name—at which every knee shall bow" (Phil. 2:9, 10). That there is a very real power in the Name, anyone associated with the healing ministry will testify. We have seen too many healed in the Name of Jesus to doubt.

In the beginning, you will do these things self-consciously, in hope. Then you will do them by rote, alternately thinking the whole thing pretty silly or a lot of superstitious nonsense. For a long time you may seem as far from your goal as when you started. And then, one day, you will know His Presence.

The means by which you have for so long laboriously tried to cultivate an awareness of Him; the meditating you have done, the prayers you have said, will no longer seem meaningless. They will have become for you a way of life—and suddenly you won't know how to live any other way. You will recognize His Hand in everything you do, and everything that happens in your life.

The night your husband comes home and tells you he got the raise, your first instinct will be to get on your knees in thanksgiving before you hoist a cocktail glass in celebration.

The day he gets his surprise promotion, you'll say, "Thank God" and mean it—not, "Boy, what a break!"

When your child's undiagnosed fever of 104 drops to normal; when the lump in your breast turns out to be a benign tumor; when your husband's chest pains are determined to be neuralgia, you won't say, "How lucky!" you'll say, "Praise the Lord!" *God* has replaced *luck* in your vocabulary.

And, curiously, you will discover, as have I and thousands before us, that the more you *consciously* acknowledge and recognize the Hand of God in your life, the more frequently it will actually be upon you in mercy and compassion. Your continual awareness of Him seems to set in motion a spiritual law as infallible as that which operates as the result of gratitude.

"Draw nigh to God, and he will draw nigh to you" (James 4:8). These words have become for you a demonstrable truth, as more and more often you feel the Presence, and are able to remain in it for increasingly long periods of time. And herein lies a hazard against which we must continually be on guard.

To know the Presence is to know God in a special and wonderful way. Once having stepped into His Presence, you will want always to be in it. You won't be alone in your emotional response, but it is something of which to be careful, for if your desire becomes too great, it can be dangerous and lead to serious emotional unbalance. Spiritual gluttony is as harmful as any other kind; and while I believe that we can't want God too much, I also believe that we can want too much of God, with the result that we may be tempted to withdraw from the rest of the world.

We resent having to descend from the mountain tops to the valleys where we must get dinner, deal with our unruly children and placate our harassed husbands. Our resentment turns to irritation at being plunged, willy nilly, from the heights to the mundane and multitudinous demands of everyday life; and we too often defeat the very cause we are trying to serve, by becoming short-tempered and irascible.

We recognize what is happening, and this recognition often serves as a psychological boomerang. It tempts us to gaze with an uneasy longing into what may seem, at this point, the spiritual pleasures of a segregated life, where we will no longer be victims of the nerve-wracking distractions of everyday living—and therefore no longer subject to the tension-induced sins of which we know ourselves guilty, but seem unable to control.

This is the sort of attitude we must at all costs avoid, for it degrades our dedication to Christ into a neurotic religiosity which is contrary to His will and far afield from Him whom we profess to want to know and serve.

From the beginning, God has worked through men, and Christianity is a faith relevant to, and for the vast majority of us, best demonstrated in, the world at large.

Jesus commands us to love Him with all our hearts, but *also* our neighbors. He never said to withdraw from them that we might worship Him the better.

To seal up our faith within ourselves; to so jealously clasp it to us that we refuse to share it and therefore to demonstrate it, is to evade the responsibility He has placed upon us as His followers.

"Ye are the light of the world," He said. "Let your light so shine before men that they may see your good works, and glorify your Father which is in heaven" (Matt. 5:16).

By the power of the Holy Spirit through prayer and worship, our individual spiritual batteries are recharged—but unless we reach out to others with the light thus generated, we hide it under a bushel. God cannot be glorified in the ensuing darkness.

To attempt to offer ourselves to Him as solitary and attenuated spiritual beings, is both futile and unrealistic; for at best, and regardless of our effort, this cannot result in sinlessness, but only in the mutilation of our humanity. Our offering thus becomes less than He created—a sacrifice on our terms not His, and thus unacceptable.

"First give thyself to God," says St. Augustine; "then to the work God gives thee to do."

Much as some of us might like to get away from the sort of work God seems to have given us; much as some of us might like at times to find asylum from the harassing, energy-consuming trivialities of everyday existence, retreat is not the answer, nor escapism the solution. The road to holiness is not that easy; nor the way to sanctity that simple.

"In as much as ye have done it unto one of the least of these my brethren," He tells us, "ye have done it unto me" (Matt. 25:45).

Our Lord makes it abundantly clear that the infinite must be attained through the finite; the eternal reached through the temporal, and the spiritual manifested through the physical.

Our mission, then, is to spread the good news that He lives and heals— not to bask alone in secret knowledge.

It is to fight evil in His Name, at the level on which it exists and we were created—not to retire to the rarefied atmosphere of an isolated and euphoric spirituality.

It is in letting Him shine through, direct and hallow our

everyday work, whatever it is and in whatever environment He
has placed us, that we may bear most telling witness to Him.
In seeking paths in which He has not led us, we are, however
unwittingly, super-imposing our wills upon His. In trying to
separate ourselves from humanity, we are, however unintentionally, separating ourselves from God, and thus inadvertently removing ourselves from the current of His sanctifying
grace.

It may seem that I unnecessarily stress the danger of what,
after all, does not seem a too-prevalant hazard in our twentieth
century culture: an excess of spiritual zeal. I freely acknowledge that this tendency does not pose a problem in most areas
of the faith where the problem is likely to be just the reverse.
However, contrary to some critics of the healing ministry who
fear that concern with the physical may take precedence over
the spiritual, I believe that it is in the healing field that there
is most frequently an inclination toward spiritual over-em-
phasis. This is not due to fanaticism, but rather to the fact
that this ministry is so peculiarly pervaded by the Presence of
Christ, and those who participate so closely and continually
surrounded by the evidence of His love and mercy, that there
can easily develop a reluctance to step out of His Light into
the comparative darkness of the world at large.

Many of us need reminding from time to time, that as
Christians we must live always in two worlds simultaneously,
the spiritual and the physical. It is imperative that a sane balance between the two be struck and maintained. To emphasize one at the expense of the other must inevitably result in
a maimed personality, rendering us unworthy of our discipleship; and both nullifying the meaning and negating the lesson
of the Incarnation.

Having known the Presence, if only once and only for an
instant, you will always remember how it was. Neither your
heart nor your mind will ever again be restless in the old way.
You will have found peace. And yet, in one tiny corner of

your being, there will reside for as long as you shall live, or so
it seems to me, a yearning which cannot be entirely satisfied
in this life—for once having known God in this way, you can
never have enough of Him.

People speak of "finding" God. Once having known His
Presence, you have, in a sense, "found" Him; but paradoxically, at the same time the seeking, or perhaps more accurately, the straining towards Him, seems not to abate, but often
to be intensified. As the Psalmist says: "Like as the hart panteth after the water-brooks, so panteth my soul after thee, O
God."

We have often to remind ourselves that "flesh and blood
cannot inherit the Kingdom"—and we cannot on this earth
receive Him all. Yet the desire for God in His entirety per-
sists. This longing to know and be close to Him, accompanied
by the knowledge that we can never know Him well enough
or be sufficiently close, constitutes that curious coupling of
suffering and joy which is indigenous to the Christian faith.
But it cannot be palliated by retreating to an ivory tower
which is not our intended dwelling place. As Henry Drum-
mond writes: "Talent develops itself in solitude—the talent
of prayer, of faith, of meditation, of seeing the unseen. But
character grows in the stream of the world's life."

And it is in this stream, amidst people, in each of whom we
can find something of the God we seek, that most of us are
destined to live as best we can to His glory, doing our parts
to advance His Kingdom.

Chapter 10

"fear not, neither be dismayed"

Deut. 31:8

I have spoken of cultivating an awareness of the Presence of God, and cautioned against the possibility of going spiritually overboard once we have learned to enter the Presence. But there is another factor which is equally relevant to our conscious contact with God, which concerns the apparent *loss* of that contact after it has been established.

A few weeks ago I was jarred out of sleep in the small hours of the morning by the ringing of my telephone. The voice that met mine as I lifted the receiver, was low, controlled, and unmistakably desperate. It belonged to a man in another city, suffering, I knew, from a medically incurable disease. A deeply religious man, he had at this moment come to the end of his rope—not because of his physical condition, but because he felt he had lost all contact with God.

"I feel completely forsaken and utterly hopeless." He ended by saying, "Where is this God I have worshipped? Why has He turned away from me?"

Over the centuries this question has been asked times without number, and always with much the same anguish. It stems from a sudden and insupportable sense of alienation from God.

What others in this day and age do to combat, or perhaps I should say survive, this experience, I am in no position to say. As a professional writer I am trained to research and in-

95

vestigate, but this is an area in which research is clearly im
possible; and any investigation which would necessarily com
prise interviews, would constitute an indefensible invasion o
privacy. Therefore, once again I can cite only my persona
experience in the matter, which I do with the thought, and ir
the hope that those who have not yet faced this problem, may
be better prepared to meet it with equanimity when and if i
confronts them.

Occasional periods of spiritual dryness are a common oc
currence with anyone who prays. Most of us have known many
times when our prayers seem to be discouragingly laboriou:
and barren. But I was as totally unprepared as the man whom
I have mentioned, for the first extended period of profound
and devastating spiritual desolation which suddenly assailed
me some time ago, for no apparent reason.

This was no mere "dryness." It was a terrifying sense of ir
revocable separation from God. No matter how I prayed I
could not reach Him. No matter how I sought I could not find
Him. Believing that only unrepented sin can separate us from
God, I racked my brain and conscience for days, in an effort
to unearth some sin of which I was unaware. This was to no
avail.

Although living a full and ostensibly normal life, sur
rounded by family and friends, I was actually existing for what
then seemed an eternity of time, in the greatest sense of alone
ness I have ever known. If this was a sign of spiritual de
velopment, I had only one desire: to remain always a spiritua
pygmy.

I looked back with longing to what now seemed the "good
old days" of happy paganism, and I exerted every effort to
return to them.

I tried to mentally wise-crack my way out of the impene
trable darkness in which I found myself.

I tried to convince myself that as I had successfully lived
much of my life without God, I had no need of Him now
But once having known Him, however slightly, this proved

mpossible to do. I had finally to admit the truth; for the fact
s that deep in the heart of the believer lies the conviction
which nothing can ever eradicate, that Christ lives. It is the
very *unshakableness* of this conviction which makes so shat-
tering the sense of estrangement from Him.

As time went on, my disposition grew worse. I became
nervous and irritable—the inevitable outgrowth of a profound
disorientation—and at the same time felt increasingly upset
that this was so, realizing that my reaction of itself was creat-
ing an impediment to God's love, and thus was jeopardizing
any hope of a quick reconciliation with Him.

Day after day I continued to pray (for by this time prayer
had become a deeply ingrained habit, and I no longer knew
how to live without it).

At first I pleaded for just one more moment's awareness of
Him. Refused, my prayers degenerated into tense and nerve-
racked bombardments against what seemed an impassible
stone wall. These abortive prayer attempts left me exhausted,
drenched in perspiration and feeling as physically battered as
if I had, indeed, been banging my head against an indestruct-
ible stone wall. My throat ached and my tongue was dry. I
felt, in a very real sense, as if I were dying of thirst; a thirst
which no substance on earth could relieve.

And then one day as I prayed, there seemed wrung from
my innermost being, the silent cry, "Jesus, hear me," and
simultaneously there flashed through my mind the words I
didn't even know I knew: "He liveth to make intercession for
you" (Heb. 7:25).

At that precise moment my longing became unendurable in
its intensity—and suddenly He was there. Tears flooded my
eyes in inexpressible gratitude and indescribable relief.

Much of the joy of this reconciliation was clouded by my
subsequent inability to rest and relax in God. For weeks I
lived in dread of a repetition of this experience—but as time
went on I regained my equilibrium, and could make a fairly
painless effort to fathom what had caused it all.

I suspect that these periods of spiritual desolation when the so-called "consolations" or tangible rewards of prayer are withheld, can be due to any one of a number of reasons or a combination of several.

Perhaps they are caused by an unconscious spiritual pride on our parts, because of what may have seemed the former effectiveness of our prayers; or perhaps it is simply spiritual exhaustion which is responsible. Perhaps they are the result of our spiritual gluttony—an insatiable appetite for more than we are meant to have—or perhaps they are due to the intervention of the devil, who, the closer we come to God, the more assiduously works to destroy our relationship with Him. And certainly there are times when God uses these periods as a form of discipline. Just as we attempt to teach our children to refrain from invariably greeting us with the immediate demand of "What did you bring me?" so God must be striving to teach us who so badly need to learn, to seek and love Him for Himself alone, and not His gifts.

I think it can never be a question of God deliberately withdrawing Himself from us as a punishment. "I will never leave thee nor forsake thee" (Heb. 13:5) is His promise—the promise on which our faith stands. He has never repudiated it, or us. He will never let us go from His protective care. He is always there, steadfast, unchanging and merciful. The veil of separation is never over *His* face, but only over ours. It is ultimately removed by His love and through His grace in response to our yearning for Him.

Obviously the cause or causes of our seeming estrangement from God must be largely a matter of conjecture, but the result of these experiences is unquestionable: they strengthen us spiritually beyond computation.

I have learned much of their spiritual value, for my first experience was not to be the last, although never since the first time have I suffered the same sense of panic and devastation. I am able to relax now in the inestimable comfort of the believing knowledge that Christ is indeed continually making intercession; and I rest now in my heart's cognizance as well as my mind's conviction, that His promise, "Lo, I am with you alway, even unto the end of the world" (Matt. 28:20), has never been withdrawn.

To pretend that I enjoy these periods of desolation or look forward to the next would be sheer hypocrisy—but nonetheless, I have found in them a truly God-given means of establishing an ultimately closer relationship with Him than I have ever known before—one which I think could not have otherwise been possible.

It has been said by some churchmen that intercessory prayer is the highest form of prayer. In the light of personal experience I venture now to disagree, for I have learned for the first time what pure prayer can mean: prayer unconfused by emotion and unsullied by desire for any benefits for anyone—the sort of mental prayer which asks nothing and seeks nothing except to serve God more worthily. Through this type of prayer we offer Him our faith, our love and our entire confidence; and in this giving, however inadequate it may be, our insupportable sense of alienation from Him is eased. It is as if our singleness of purpose, however short-lived; and our purity of heart, however fleeting, builds a bridge between Him and us, which spans the chasm of separation. From across the abyss we hear the unmistakable echo of His words: "Fear not, for I am with thee" (Isa. 43:5).

On the day that I finally learned to pray with no sense of contact with God, I knew that I had received, unasked, what is perhaps the greatest of all His gifts—the gift of faith. Not the fighting faith which moves mountains, but the quiet trust which knows they *can* be moved. Above all else I have received, I am grateful for this trust, which is at once an impregnable shield against spiritual disaster, and a perpetual assurance against the desperation born of that once intolerable sense of separation.

People have said these periods of spiritual desolation can last as long as five years. Whether even now I could withstand five years without the consolation of His Presence I am not prepared to say. I can only hope so.

Should I ever be confronted with such an endurance contest, I must only believe that if my memory of Him should falter; or if my longing for Him should become again unbearable in its intensity, that He in His mercy will give me back, as He has before, the awareness as well as the knowledge of Himself.

Meanwhile, although I am fully cognizant that this experience will from time to time recur, I only know that I have lost all fear of what once seemed a fairly accurate foretaste of hell.

I only know that whether in conscious contact with God or not, I am unequivocally certain that He lives, and is never farther from me than the air I breathe.

"I am the Light of the world," He said. "He who follows me will not walk in darkness" (John 8:12). I have learned at last this truth.

I am well aware that at this point the unbeliever might rationally observe: "If all this suffering is involved in the Christian faith, where is the supposed joy?"

I can only answer, what every Christian knows, that it lies unquenchable in the heart of anyone who has ever known, in the smallest way, Our Lord; or felt, in the slightest degree, His Love.

It lies in the seeking as well as the knowing; in His Presence as well as in His power. It is even an inherent part of the desolation itself, which holds the promise of the ineffable joy of reunion with Him after a long time away. And most of all, perhaps, it lies in our ability to pray with St. Augustine, and at long last to mean the words we say: "Give me Thine own self, without which, though Thou shouldst give me all that ever Thou hast made, yet could not my desires be satisfied."

Chapter 11

receiving his healing power

The longer I have observed the healing ministry at work; the more cases I have investigated and had medically confirmed; the more I have experienced God in my own life, the more unequivocally certain I am that in His sight there is no incurable disease.

God does not change. As during His earthly ministry He unfailingly met people at the place of their need, whether spiritual *or* physical, so today, if you are in need of healing, you may receive it at His Hands as surely as did the multitudes who came to Him centuries ago—and your *worthiness*, as did theirs, has nothing to do with it.

A woman recently voiced a common misconception, when she said: "Spiritual healing is new to me. What can I do to earn this wonderful blessing from God?"

In the sense that she meant, the answer was "nothing." We can't *earn* our healing any more than we can earn our salvation—for healing is part of that salvation. It is not a gratuity from God for services rendered; it is a fulfillment of His will for our wholeness.

"But surely there must be *something* I should do if I am to know His healing power?" she asked with evident frustration.

This was a different question. There is much that we not only *can*, but *must* do, if we are to know the healing Christ. A clergyman with a remarkable healing ministry succinctly summed it up not long ago, when he commented: "If people only realized how easy it is to receive the healing power of God! All it takes is faith and self-relinquishment."

My only quarrel with this statement is the use of the adjective "easy." If many of us have found the acquisition of a simple faith to be prodigiously difficult, we have found self-renunciation to be scarcely less so. Surely it has never been "easy" for the average self-centered and self-interested human being to relinquish himself, and today it is more difficult than ever. One of the problems peculiar to our times is aptly expressed by a man who, after undergoing psychoanalysis for a lengthy period, finally turned in desperation to the healing ministry.

"Having been told for years," he said, "that my health depended first on 'finding' myself and then on 'expressing' myself, it was something of a switch to Christianity's demand that I 'lose' myself, and express only God. Funny thing, though" he went on, "my healing actually began on the day that I first *really* understood what Our Lord meant when He said: 'Whosoever will lose his life for my sake, the same shall save it' " (Luke 9:24).

Through the healing ministry a great many of us who have long been reluctant to surrender our egos, or as one person put it, our "individuality," have learned that it is only in fusing our identities with God that we can achieve wholeness; and only in losing ourselves to Him that we can truly "find" ourselves as individuals. But in the beginning, most of us tend to seek an easier way, as did the man who said to me the other day: "I've promised God that if He will heal me, I'll spend the rest of my life witnessing to His glory."

The trouble is, God isn't interested in striking bargains. He demands nothing less than our commitment. His healing is a gift; but although it is without price, it has a cost which for most of us is astronomically high: our lives. We must let

Him have us if He is to heal us. It is true that some are spon-
tanously healed, *after* which their lives are changed; but for
the vast majority of us, healing is contingent upon trying to
transform our lives *first*. "Except a man be born again, he cannot see the Kingdom of God" (John 3:1); nor is he apt to
feel the touch of His healing Hand.

Time and time again it has been demonstrated that relinquishment, not only of ourselves but our loved ones, is an
essential condition for healing. Take, for example, the case of
a small child who suffered medically uncontrollable seizures
due to a pre-natal brain injury. Pediatricians and neurologists
rendered a unanimous verdict of hopeless.

The grieving parents flooded the heavens with their prayers,
but apparently to no avail. Finally, at the suggestion of friends,
they consulted with a member of the healing clergy. "Release
David to God," the minister said. "Let him go so that God
can heal him in His own way." This process of "letting go," is
never easy—but with the help of the Holy Spirit through
prayer, the parents could finally say and mean it, if only for
a few minutes at a time in the beginning: "Lord, we commend David to your care, knowing that you love him even
more than we do. We give him to you now, confident that
what you do for him is right and good." Gradually these brief
periods of relinquishment extended, so that for days at a time
they could commend their son to God in confidence. The
child's health immediately began to improve, and today he is
normal in every respect.

In a very real sense, the essence of the healing ministry is
to be found in the words: "Release and ye shall be released"
(Luke 6:37, Amplified Version). Release your fear and anxiety to God, and you are liberated from them. Release your
resentment and hostility, and you are freed from them. Release yourself to Him, and you can be healed, as was a woman
suffering from a medically hopeless disease, who a year ago
sought spiritual healing. For months nothing seemed to hap-

pen, and then one day she asked me to see her. She was bed-ridden and in shocking physical condition, but there was a new light in her eyes. "I may not have been physically healed," she said, "but I feel like a different person. Last week, for the first time, I was able to completely surrender myself to God—and I've been praying ever since that sick or well, He would somehow use me to advance the Kingdom." I saw this woman last week at a healing service. She is now working a full eight-hour day without fatigue.

The difference between surrender to God and capitulation to the evil of sickness is a subtle one, but all-important. The prayer of relinquishment is never in conflict with the prayer of faith, nor is it a substitute. It is the climax of your prayer for healing—the offering of your life to Him in service, that whatever the circumstances, you may live to His glory.

The cost of discipleship is high, and for many of us the discipline exacted by the healing ministry is arduous. Not the least of its problems in our over-busy lives, is that of *time*.

Not long ago a woman, after professing her great desire for spiritual growth, remarked: "I've only time for a quick prayer after I'm in bed, and I usually fall asleep in the middle of *that*."

She expressed a typical human inconsistency. We all concede that proficiency in any field requires the expenditure of time and effort; yet almost universally, we except matters of the spirit, where the reward is not merely proficiency, but God. We all have many time-consuming interests, yet it is only when He matters above all else, that we can learn to know Him. Few of us can spend unlimited hours in undisturbed prayer, but nevertheless, we can "pray without ceasing" (1 Thess. 5:17). What is essential is a constant awareness of God; a continual effort to glorify Him in whatever we do. The more time we spend with Him, the more we receive of Him; and the closer we live to Him, the more discernibly are we indwelt by Him.

Until we love Him more than ourselves, we will lack the desire for total commitment. Unless we are *conscious* of His enabling love for us, we must lack the fortitude to relinquish ourselves; for such relinquishment can sometimes be as painful as physical death, or so it seems to me. It means a willing dying of self that "He may increase while we decrease" (John 3:30); and this for many of us, means a continuous "killing" of self that the Holy Spirit may come alive in us. It means a ceaseless attempt to subjugate our wills to His; a continual process of uprooting destructive emotions. It means for many, as for me, the painful annihilation of personal ambition, selfishness and pride—and the courage to face our endless failure. In short, it means a perpetual battle to over-ride the forces of evil which constantly seek to drive us from Him, so that some day we may be able to say with some semblance of truth: "I live; yet not I, but Christ liveth in me" (Gal. 2:20).

We undertake this task joyfully, because of what we think to be our knowledge of God; and find that, paradoxically, our effort proves the way by which we finally come to know Him—and thus at last to share in the glory of the Resurrection as He means us to.

On a recent sight-seeing tour of the house of a religious Order, I was shown their prayer list. At the top was inscribed: "We beseech Thee to heal—if it be Thy will." I said nothing, but my guide must have read my expression, for he asked: "Is this the wrong way to pray for the sick?" Feeling extremely presumptuous, I could only explain that we believe that the qualifying phrase, "If it be Thy will," has no place in healing prayer. When we pray for guidance, we seek to learn the will of God. When we pray for healing we assume, on the authority of Jesus, that we know it.

I think that no prayer goes unheard, but through the healing ministry, we have learned that *how* we pray, does indeed matter.

Time without number we have seen that prayer for healing,

offered with reservations as to God's will, is a prayer without power because it is a prayer offered with less than complete faith.

A year ago a man suffered a massive brain hemorrhage. Forty-three years old and given but a short time to live, I was called to the hospital at his request. His wife met me at the door saying; "He's in coma now. His death is the will of God." I had only time to demur, and ask that she pray with me, with all the confidence that she could summon, that he be healed according to God's will; meanwhile envisioning her husband, not as the comatose figure on the bed, but vigorous and whole. I laid on hands, and midway through the healing prayer, I felt the patient stir. At the end of the prayer, he joined us in the "amen." He was to leave the hospital ten days later. Coincidence? No—there have been too many such cases. Why? In healing prayer, as in every aspect of the Faith, we are compelled, as St. Augustine says, to "Here believe; there understand."

"Therefore I tell you, whatever you ask in prayer, believe that you receive it, and you will" (Mark 11:24 RSV). To *believe* your healing even before physical evidence of it; to give thanks even before it is accomplished (John 11:41); to pray with the conviction that what you ask in His Name will be done (John 15:16); these are the acts of faith required of you; the indispensable conditions of your healing, which cannot be met by any process of rationalization, but only by the grace of the Holy Spirit, realizable through prayer.

"Let him ask in faith, nothing wavering. For he that wavereth is like a wave of the sea, driven with the wind, and tossed. For let not that man think that he shall receive anything of the Lord" (James 1:6, 7).

But what about praying for loved ones? "I can't *help* being afraid," said the distressed wife of a critically ill man. "My prayers are bound to 'waver.'"

It is true that if we *completely* believed in the power and mercy of God, none of us would ever pray an anxious or a worried prayer. But Our Lord lived among men. He knows the impossibility of an always-unfaltering faith. A merciful God surely forgives and understands that our anxiety for those we love means not that our faith is less, but that just for a little while, our love is more.

One of the most infallible spiritual laws is that operative in an attitude of thanksgiving. "Rejoice evermore—in everything give thanks—for this is the will of God" (1 Thess. 5:16, 18). It is also one of the ways His will is fulfilled in us.

About a year ago, a man said bitterly: "It would be sheer hypocrisy for me to offer thanksgiving. Am I supposed to be *grateful* that I've been laid off—and that the worry has caused my ulcer to get so bad the doctor says I have to be operated on?"

Later on that evening, the man grudgingly conceded that regardless of his circumstances, he still had much to be thankful for.

I saw him the other day. "I decided to try out what you said," he told me. "Long before I went back to work I tried to begin each day by saying: 'This is the day the Lord hath made; I will rejoice and be glad in it' (Psalm 118:24). Finally I began to really mean it. It's fantastic, but this small thing has transformed my life—and incidentally, my ulcer is healed."

To go to God with grateful hearts is never hypocrisy or Pollyanna fatuousness. It is to set in motion a spiritual law. When thanksgiving becomes an intrinsic part of your life, a curious thing invariably happens; there is more and more to be grateful *for*. And transcending all else, is the abiding knowledge that nothing and no one can ever take from us what we have of God.

If all kinds of prayer but one were to be taken from me, I should ask to retain the prayer of thanksgiving. Through this prayer, which begins at the foot of the Cross, we are uplifted by the Holy Spirit, who leads us through gratitude into worship and that "Joy of the Lord which is our strength" (Neh. 8:10): a strength which permeates every cell of our bodies; a perceptible power which prevails against tension and fatigue and sickness, and before which the forces of evil seem to shrink and recede.

If I were permitted but one petition, it would be that of George Herbert*: "Thou hast given so much to us, give us one thing more—a grateful heart."

About two years ago a woman confronted me with a problem which until then I had not faced. Since that time her situation, with various ramifications, has presented itself with sufficient frequency to warrant attention here.

When I first saw this woman, she suffered from a far-advanced, and extensively metastasized malignancy. Until a few weeks before, she had resigned herself to inevitable death. Then the healing ministry came to her attention for the first time. She subsequently became convinced that her illness was not, in fact, God's will—and with this new conviction she became confused. She spent her dwindling strength in travelling around the country, frantically attending one healing service after another—and felt increasingly guilty because she was not quickly healed. I spent many hours with her before she got straightened out.

If you by chance find yourself in a like situation, don't let your new certainty that God's will for you is health, start you on the heretical road to believing that the healing of your body is *all* that matters, and that *you* are responsible for it. Your physical healing is important, but the *most* important thing is that you grow closer and closer to God. The nearer you come to Him, the better you will comprehend what at first glance appears to be an irreconcilable paradox: namely, God's will for you is health and you must seek it by every means at your command; but it is when you realize with your heart that if only you can know Him better than you ever

* 17th Century Anglican divine.

have before, you don't *care* whether or not you are physically healed, that you are most likely to receive healing. In this sense it will come to you unsought; and this holds true for all of us. It is when our spirit thirsts for God more avidly than our body craves healing, that we can receive Him—and as a corollary, His healing grace.

For those of us blessed with good health, this is an easy dictum. For those who are not, it can be incredibly difficult—and many is the time I have felt intolerably presumptuous in enunciating it to someone in great pain, when the desire for relief involuntarily takes precedence over everything else. The saving factor is that no matter what the illness, there are always moments when the pain decreases in intensity.

A few months ago, for example, a woman who knew little of spiritual healing, asked me to see her husband who was suffering intense pain from cancer. While it is true that through prayer and the sacramental healing rites pain, which drugs can't touch, is often alleviated whether or not the patient is familiar with the healing ministry, I think that whenever possible the patient should be instructed, however briefly, *before* receiving the healing rite, if for no other reason than to obviate any suggestion of magic. In this case I arranged my visit shortly after he had received sedation so that he would be sufficiently pain-free to understand what I was saying.

I was not surprised to find him extraordinarily responsive. A quick and profound comprehension by the desperate is a frequently bestowed mercy of God.

After the healing prayer, the patient said: "For just a flash I wanted God more than anything else in the world, but the next minute all I could think of was being healed." Nevertheless, it was at this moment that he wanted God more than His favors, that his healing actually began. He has since received the laying on of hands six times. After each ministration he has remained longer without pain. He is now walking and requires no sedation whatsoever.

God yearns to bestow His healing upon us as much as we long to receive it, but although we are saved by faith (Gal. 2:16), we must also fulfill the law.

"I am the way, the truth and the life," He said (John 14:6). "Follow thou me" (John 21:22). I believe these words constitute a summary of the law of healing. You will sometimes weary of stumbling and falling times without number in your attempt to follow Him, but all He asks is your persistence. You have His promise that "he that shall endure unto the end, the same shall be saved" (Mark 13:13).

Each time you fall, He in His mercy returns to your side to raise you up—and each time this happens, the Light seems to glow a little more brightly and comes a little bit nearer, until you find yourself within its arc. You have stepped into His healing Light, not by will power but by grace; not by affirmative thinking, but by faith.

In an era when knowledge is more often glorified than God, it has taken many of us a long time to learn that knowledge is not sanctity. In an age when the mind is more frequently worshipped than its Creator, it has taken many of us a long time to admit with Thomas à Kempis, that only "he that doeth the will of God is truly learned."

But as at last we know the truth with more than our intellects, we find that it has, indeed, set us free. We are ready now to receive the total salvation He offers us: wholeness of body, mind and spirit.

"And this is the confidence that we have in Him; that if we ask anything according to His will, He heareth us: and if we know that He hear us, we know that we have the petitions that we desired of Him" (1 John 5:14, 15).

Chapter 12

"when ye pray"

Luke 11:2

Recently a woman asked a question which I have heard voiced innumerable times, and not always by professed unbelievers.

"If God is all-knowing," she said, "why waste your time on prayer? Presumably He doesn't need *you* to tell Him the need. Besides, as long as He'll do what He wants anyway, what's the point of always saying, 'Let Thy will be done'?"

God gave many of us, myself included, inquiring minds—but if there is one thing I have learned over the past few years, it is this: there are certain areas in which strict obedience is required of us, and it matters not at all whether we understand or agree. Prayer is one of these areas. God has ordained that through prayer He shall work in our lives. We can't rationalize this, and we can't put ourselves in the position of arguing with Him. It is one of His inviolable laws, which if we want His Presence and His power, we must obey.

It is entirely true that God knows our need before we express it. "Your Father knoweth what things ye have need of before ye ask Him." "Before they call, I will answer" (Matt. 6:8, Isa. 65:24). We pray not to instruct or inform God, but as an act of faith that we may know better what he requires of us. We pray, not in order to alter *His* will, but to bring *ourselves* into accordance with it. We pray not necessarily to bring things to pass, but rather to bring the things of the Kingdom into our cognizance. "Whatsoever God doeth, it shall be forever; nothing can be put to it, nor anything taken from it" (Eccl. 3:14). Obviously we can't change God—but through prayer He miraculously changes us.

Not long ago a man commented: "Prayer is certainly a wonderful thing. For years I have detested the man I work for. Circumstances got so bad that a few months ago I decided in desperation to try praying and see if anything would happen. It certainly did! Today we are the best of friends. How God has changed him!"

What actually occurred here is that God changed the one who prayed. I have frequently had this same experience of disliking certain people; of finding certain circumstances almost unbearably difficult. When, as the result of prayer, my dislike has turned to genuine affection, and formerly untenable situations no longer seem bothersome, I have come to recognize that the change wrought by God is in me and my attitude —and not in the other fellow or the circumstances.

A few weeks past I heard a clergyman speak on prayer. His text was "Lord, teach us to pray" (Luke 11:1); his thesis, that the disciples' request was to teach us *to* pray, which is all-important; not *how* to pray, which is something no one should need to learn. Up to a certain point, this is undoubtedly true. I don't believe that any prayer from the heart has ever been wasted; and I also believe that in this "how to" age, many of us concerned with prayer tend to overemphasize its techniques. It is quite possible to become so involved with the "hows" that our prayers take on the characteristics of a cake recipe: so much of this, so much of that; combine ingredients and cook (pray) for thirty minutes. So punctiliously followed directions may result in a good cake, but not necessarily in effective prayer.

Nevertheless, my clergyman friend erred in quoting his text out of context; for Jesus explicitly answered the disciples' question by telling them *exactly how* to pray, when He gave them, and us, the Lord's Prayer (Luke 11:2). We sometimes tend to forget that this is the model prayer, and relegate it to the place of mere rote, to be mumbled nightly as we fall asleep, which frequently happens before we get to the "amen."

Not surprisingly, there is contained in this prayer the elements of all prayer, including healing. "Thy Kindom come, Thy will be done on earth as it is in heaven," might well serve as our basic prayer of faith, for in this single phrase is all we really need to know of healing prayer. It is the statement of our belief that the will of God is always for our good; and when it is done on earth it means not calamity as we seem invariably to expect whenever we say "Thy will be done," but the unspeakably wonderful things of His Kindom, realized. When we change our attitude to recognize this; to expect the best and not the worst, we will no longer pray fearfully, "Heal me, God, *if* it be Thy will"; but confidently, "Heal me, God, *according* to Thy will that I should be well and strong and at peace." The difference here is infinitely more than the changing of one small word. It is the difference between an attitude of despair and one of victory.

When we first begin to pray, most of us do so with the intent of "using" God for our own ends. We proffer Him only a slightly different version of our childhood petition: "Please God don't let it rain tomorrow and spoil our picnic." But as through our prayer efforts we grow closer to Him; as we begin to understand that He has indeed "loved us with an everlasting love" (Jer. 31:3); as we begin to know with our hearts that "as the Father hath loved me, so have I loved you" (John 15:9), we strive perhaps for the first time to actively continue in His love. It is then that our prayers change, and we begin to pray that *He* use *us* to His glory and not to our convenience.

"Never ask God to use you unless you really mean it," someone said to me once. I know now what he meant, for once praying this prayer with your heart, He will take over your entire life, using you in ways and with a fullness which you cannot now even begin to imagine. A successful business man, for example, gives up his career to work full-time in the Camps Farthest Out*; a woman of great wealth dedicates her life to working with defective children; a brilliant physicist takes perpetual vows in a lay religious order; and so it has been with countless others.

Since the time of St. James, who established the format of the healing ministry, and said: "And the prayer of faith shall save the sick" (James 5:15), we have come to associate "the prayer of faith" with prayer for the sick—but obviously *every* prayer we speak must be a prayer of faith or it is powerless.

"The Lord shall guide thee continually" (Isa. 58:11) is a promise which only the believer claims, and in the claiming he finds it fulfilled in a thousand mundane, as well as more significant, ways. From finding a parking space on a busy street, to the culmination of a vital business deal; from the buying of a new dress, to the making of important, far-reaching decisions; from cooking a meal, to determining the course of our lives, the Lord does indeed guide us if we will only pause long enough to listen.

As the habit of prayer grows, so does our awareness of God, until actually we *do* "pray without ceasing," reaching the point where, quite literally, we do not walk across the room without being somehow conscious of Him.

It is this continuous consciousness of God—of itself a form of prayer—which changes our lives more than any other one thing, or so it has seemed to me. By it we are led from one level of prayer to the next. As in all matters of the spirit, we progress according to our desire to reach God. As we come to each plateau we rest awhile, temporarily content with what we have—and then our hearts begin again to "cry out for the living God" (Psalm 84:2); and in response, He lifts us to the next stage. Each time we come just a little nearer to Him.

* A witnessing prayer movement sounded by GLENN CLARK, in 1930.

To know that in prayer we may contact God, that by it we are brought into His Presence, and through it we may receive His power, seems to me a continually recurring miracle.

Although prayer formulas can be useful and I have myself offered them, I have come increasingly to feel that once we thoroughly understand the purpose of prayer, dogmatism is both unnecessary and out of place except as regards two all-encompassing fundamentals which experience has proved should be observed.

First, concerning healing: the strongly affirmative prayer for healing requires for many an entirely new approach to prayer. We have so long been accustomed to stating our need and then sanctimoniously quavering: "If it be Thy will," that to positively declare: "In the Name of Jesus, claim your healing," smacks to some of irreverency; while to assert boldly: "In His Name be thou whole," seems to others outright blasphemy.

Yet the truth is that Jesus in His earthly ministry gave us the pattern for healing prayer—a pattern followed by the apostles and practised ever since by His healing disciples. To insert an equivocal phrase indicates in most cases not so much a commendable acquiescence to God's will as a lamentable lack of faith; not so much submission to His Authority, as lack of trust.

The basic fundamental of all prayer consists of the five so-called essential points: worship, thanksgiving, repentance, intercession and petition. The inclusion of all these factors soon becomes instinctive in our every approach to God. As our prayer opens with adoration, we are inevitably led into thanksgiving for Him whom we worship. As our hearts kneel before Him, we are assailed by a sense of our own unworthiness and spontaneously we implore His absolution that we may remain in the Presence of His complete Holiness. Receiving it, we translate our gratitude into expressible human terms and offer our prayers for others. Lastly, we petition Him for our own needs, great or small.

Our soul has magnified the Lord (BCP, p. 26) and we have indeed come before His Presence with thanksgiving (BCP, p. 9).

Beyond these widely inclusive imperatives of prayer, I must believe that it matters little whether we pray aloud or silently; the exact words we say; whether we use "Thee" or "You" when addressing God. For the "Kingdom of God is not in word but in power" (1 Cor. 4:20).

What *does* matter above all else, is the attitude of our hearts, for this alone determines the effectiveness of prayer, and in turn, the power we receive from God.

One meaning of the word "prayer"*—a meaning with which too many of us have for too long been totally unfamiliar—is "joyous expectation"; a joy which is often too deep for superficial gaity but sometimes overflows into tears; an expectancy which is not idle dreaming, but an abiding confidence in the validity of His promise: "Have faith in God," He said, "for whosoever shall say unto this mountain, Be thou removed, and be thou cast into the sea; and *shall not doubt* in his heart, but shall believe that those things which he saith shall come to pass; he shall have whatsoever he saith" (Mark 11:22-23).

These qualities of joy and expectancy, both of which are born of faith, seem to me completely indispensable in any kind of prayer offered for any cause whatsoever; and the fact that they are so seldom present, either singly or in combination, may well account for the fact that our prayers seem so often impotent.

Recently a woman said to me: "I guess my trouble is that I expect too much of God." Whatever her trouble may be, I know it is not that. None of us can ever expect too much of God. Our besetting sin, and I think it *is* a sin, is that we habitually expect so pitifully little, daring to impose upon His mercy and His power, the limits of our own humanity.

---

* In both Old and New Testament there are several words which have different meanings in the original tongue, but all have been translated as "prayer."

"All things that are mine are thine, and thine are mine" (John 17:10) in His assurance. "Verily, verily I say unto you, whatsoever ye shall ask the Father in My Name, He will give it to you" (John 16:23) is His promise. How, then, *can* we expect too much?

As I believe we should not be dogmatic about the *words* we say in prayer, neither, I think, should we be arbitrary about the *way* in which to pray.

To me, for example, it seems important to pray as often as I am able, in the same place; but to others this doesn't matter at all. Many advisors on prayer advocate a relaxed and comfortable sitting position, especially for meditation; but I happen to prefer to pray on my knees, although I haven't always. But although Paul says: "On bended knee I pray the Father" (Eph. 3:14), I doubt that our physical posture makes much difference to God. Our spirits kneel before Him in prayer regardless of the position of our bodies.

Nevertheless, I was interested when a clergyman stopped by several months ago to discuss a problem, and ended by saying: "You know, I think the difficulty may lie in the fact that I haven't done enough praying *on my knees* of late. I intend to remedy that situation today."

Last week I saw this minister again. "I'm sure I don't know why it should be so," he said, "but I've found that *kneeling* when I pray seems to make an almost incredible difference." Could it be that after all we *should* kneel before the throne of Grace? Perhaps.

We who are parents often deplore the fact that our children so seldom seem able to learn from *our* experience passed on by word of mouth, but must find out certain things for themselves through trial and error. For me, and probably for many adults, the same thing seems to obtain in the field of the spirit. Regardless of teaching and our intellectual acceptance of certain truths, unless we personally experience them, we cannot wholly comprehend them.

"Set your mind on things that are above, not on the things

that are on the earth" (Col. 3:2 RSV). These words do not deny our earthly needs; they point the way to their fulfillment. Only relatively recently have I discovered for myself the extent to which our physical needs are met when we focus our hearts entirely on the Kingdom and our hopes primarily on spiritual favors.

From the beginning I have recognized that "God is a Spirit, and they that worship Him must worship Him in spirit and in truth" (John 4:24). From the beginning I have realized that "If we live in the Spirit, we must also walk in the Spirit" (Gal. 5:25). But it is only now that I have come to fully know what it means to *really* pray by the Spirit, for the Spirit. As I have learned to pray, for others as well as for myself, not for physical benefits alone, but most fervently for spiritual blessings, I have discovered that a curious phenomenon occurs. As in Holy Communion the *material* forms of the bread and wine mystically become the spiritual food of the Body and Blood of Our Lord, so, conversely, are the spiritual blessings for which we pray, mysteriously converted into the practical necessities for this earthly life.

To be granted a "mighty increase of strength by His Spirit"; to know the "love of Christ which surpasses all knowledge"; to be "filled with the entire fullness of God" (Eph. 3:16, 19), is the answer to our every need—the assurance of complete wholeness.

For me, then, these words of Paul have become the basic foundation, holding the key to the power, of all petitionary and intercessory prayer—the prayer which we conclude with Paul: "Now to him who by the power at work within us is able to do far more abundantly than all that we ask or think, to Him be glory in the church and in Christ Jesus to all generations, for ever and ever" (Eph. 3:20, 21 RSV).

This is the climax of our petition, in which we seek with confident expectation, the fulfillment of *all* our needs, above all that we ask or even *think*, giving God the praise and the glory that this should be so. To pray otherwise, has become, for me, to "ask amiss."

"In nothing be anxious; but in everything by prayer and supplication with thanksgiving, let your requests be made known unto God" (Phil. 4:6).

All of us do not pray in the same way; but each of us who prays, whether we are taking our first tentative step toward God, or whether we kneel, grateful beyond the telling, in His Presence, may be sure of one thing: "The Lord is nigh unto all that call upon Him," and "He shall supply all your need according to His riches in Christ Jesus" (Psalm 145:18, Phil. 4:19).

Chapter 13

"brethren, pray for us"

Anyone who has ever been on the receiving end of intercessory prayer knows what it can mean. He knows that to be upheld in prayer is not merely a vaguely comforting thought; it is to receive a very real and tangible strength.

In travelling around the country I have acquired an unusually long prayer list, for wherever I go, people ask for prayer. But it works both ways, for a great many place *me* on *their* prayer lists, which means that hundreds of people, most of whom I don't know, are praying for me. No one but God knows how grateful I am that this is so, for I think we are all desperately in need of each other's prayers, and none of us can ever have enough—not only in times of particular crisis, but throughout our daily lives.

A thousand times I have felt the effects of these prayers at the most unlikely times. Often while walking down the street, or sitting in a theater, or shopping, or preparing dinner, I have suddenly known that wonderful elevation of the spirit; that flooding with inexplicable joy; that surge of vitality, which are the result of prayer.

So undeniable is the impact, yet in the beginning so incredible did the whole thing seem to me, that I used to check back whenever possible; and time after time I would discover that at the precise time that I had experienced these reactions, someone was in prayer for me.

I have never got entirely used to this remarkable phenom-enon, and even now occasionally fail to connect the result with the cause. Take for example the past six months, during which I have been working very hard. The end of each day custom-arily finds me extremely tired, except, curiously enough, on one night a week. For a long time I paid no attention to this, at-tributing it to the fact that the day must have been an easier one than usual. It was not until someone asked me to do some-thing on a Friday evening and I found myself asking: "Could you possibly make it on Wednesday instead?", that I con-sciously realized that it was always on *Wednesday*, regardless of what I was doing after dinner, that I felt a tremendous surge of vitality run through me, which lasted until bedtime.

The other night, on a Wednesday, I happened to go to a healing service in an outlying church—one in which I had not been since I had spoken there some months before. As I knelt in a rear pew, I heard my name read from the altar, and God's blessing asked for me and my work.

No one knew that I was in the church that night, and I had no idea that I was on that particular church's prayer list. I was to discover later that my name had been permanently placed there six months before. This, then, was the explana-tion of my mid-week energy!

No one knows better than I how absurd this sort of thing can sound—or how unbelievable; but again and again it happens.

Take the day I felt so spiritually drained after long periods of prayer for a close relative, that I asked my rector to pray not only for the patient but also for me. The prayers con-cluded, I went back to work, and within minutes felt such a joyous soaring of my heart and such a sense of spiritual strength and repleteness, that I dropped my pencil and paused in momentary wonderment before I realized what it was.

The one for whom we had offered prayer, remarked that night: "Someone must have prayed for me this afternoon at about four o'clock. Something happened then, and I've felt marvellously better ever since." Coincidence? As John Coburn, Dean of the Episcopal Seminary in Cambridge, puts it: "All I know is that when you pray for someone 'coincidences' like this happen. When you don't, these 'coincidences' stop." The results of the first controlled scientific experiment in prayer therapy, conducted by Dr. Wm. R. Parker, psychologist of the University of Redlands, give added validity to the Dean's observation.

Most of us tend to *react* rather than *act*. No matter how happy and exuberant we may feel, let us meet someone who is depressingly disagreeable, and our inclination is to react by being disagreeable in return. Through prayer, we can *act*. Having myself so often received the inestimable benefits of intercessory prayer I began some time ago, both as an experiment and in the hope of bringing comfort, to pray for strangers. This has been a fascinating venture, often evoking fantastic results.

In one instance I recall a particularly sullen and uncooperative taxi driver. Annoyed, I instinctively started to react in the way I have described—by being equally disagreeable. And then, more as a game than anything else, I said a short prayer for him. The change in his attitude was instantaneous. He became jovial and talkative, and as we entered the street of my destination, he turned off his meter with a block yet to go. As I got out of the cab I said: "God bless you the rest of the day." He grinned and replied: "He already has. I don't know why, but I suddenly feel wonderful!"

Or take the case of an extremely surly waitress in a restaurant where a friend and I had gone for dinner before time to catch my plane. "Let's move to another table and get another waitress," said my friend. I started to acquiesce, then thought better of it. "I know this sounds ridiculous," I said, "but let's just pray for this woman for a minute and see what happens."

Within three minutes, the waitress emerged from the

kitchen carrying our orders, which she had said couldn't be prepared in less than half an hour. She was a metamorphosized person, wreathed now in smiles, and unable to do enough to please us for the remainder of the meal.

In the certain knowledge that prayer brings solace, it has become my custom to pray for the bereaved whenever a funeral procession passes; for the occupant of the ambulance which shrieks down the street; the worried-looking woman in the A and P; the drunk staggering outside the bar; the lame man a few houses down whom I don't know but often see laboriously walking up the hill. I believe that somehow these people will feel the power of prayer and be helped, as I know was the man who last summer had the room adjoining ours in a resort hotel. He had recently been in a serious automobile accident, and as a consequence, suffered nightmares when his screams could be heard all over that floor of the hotel.

I began to pray that he might know the peace of God, and he quieted almost at once. Each time thereafter that he began to scream, I repeated my prayer, until finally he slept all through the night without disturbance.

Having seen prayer work so remarkably in relatively unimportant spheres as well as in really significant ones, I can only wonder that our churches do not utilize the tremendous prayer power which lies latent within them. In times of disaster, such as floods or hurricanes; or airplane accidents or train wrecks or any headlined catastrophic event involving people which is brought to our attention, I could wish that every one of our churches would offer prayer on Sunday mornings for the survivors. We cannot compute the comfort, the strength, the peace that it might bring—and it would take such a little time and effort to do.

How to pray for the old and sick is a recurring question. This must be a matter of guidance, for circumstances alter cases, but perhaps a partial answer can be found in an incident which occurred a year or so ago.

A friend in another city telephoned me one morning at ? A.M. to ask prayer for her mother, who was 85 years old. She was suffering from a degenerative brain disease, out of her mind, and screaming for hours on end in what appeared to be agony, although the doctor denied she was in pain. "I simply had to call you now" said my friend, apologizing for the hour. "I couldn't stand those screams another minute." I didn't wonder, for their sound as they came through the telephone chilled my blood.

There was no medical hope of recovery, nor even of imminent death—for the patient's heart was unusually strong, and the doctor's prediction was that she would continue on in the same condition for many months.

I suggested to my friend, as coherently as I was able at that hour of the morning, how she might pray, and assured her that I would be praying with her.

The phone had awakened my husband, so I told him the story, and we prayed together, something to this effect: "Lord, let the knowledge and love of God fill the heart and soul and subconscious mind of thy servant, Alice, alleviating all her distress, and bringing her the peace which only You can bring. Believing that it is according to Thy will, we ask that you take her quickly and peacefully into Thy Kingdom, that she may receive the complete healing which your near Presence alone can bestow. We ask this in Thy Name, believing that it is done. We commit her now, with faith, into Thy protective care."

At 7 A.M. my friend called again to say that within ten minutes after her first telephone call, her mother had stopped screaming, and with a beatific smile on her face had lapsed into her final quiet sleep.

This friend of mine had never before really believed in prayer, and had actually called me about her mother in sheer desperation, which I well knew. However, about a month later as I was leaving the house at noon to fly East, I received from

...er a Special Delivery letter asking prayers for someone who
was critically ill.

The next evening I met my friend for dinner. "Thank
heaven you got my letter in time!" were her opening words.
As I hadn't mentioned receiving the letter, I asked what she
meant. "It's obvious you were praying for Doris," she said.
"She rallied remarkably yesterday at about one in the afternoon." Then as an afterthought, she asked: "What time did
you get my letter, anyway?" When I told her, she just nodded.
"That's what I figured," she said.

A great many people have asked about praying for the sick
children of unbelievers. One such query came from a Christian
man, who sought healing for his small niece, whom he idol-
ized; the daughter of his only sister, who was an agnostic.

"Will the agnosticism of her parents impede Ann's healing?" he asked. In view of what I have observed, I had to
answer that in my opinion it could hinder, although certainly
not necessarily prevent, her healing. I believe that the faith
of the patient is of paramount importance. If the patient is
unconscious or mentally deranged, the faith may be subconscious and will still be an activating factor. Next in importance, in all cases, is the faith of the family, who love the
most; and finally, the faith of the administering clergyman.
Any dereliction of faith in any of these is a handicap—to have
the dereliction in the immediate family is a serious, although
by no means insuperable, impediment.

The uncle in this case had prayed long and fervently for
the child's recovery, and then, upon my advice, and with the
permission of the child's parents, he took her to a number of
healing services. There was no discernible physical improvement.

"I simply can't understand," he said, "why God doesn't
dramatically heal Ann so as to convince her parents of His
reality." My only reply to this could be that according to *our*
light, this would certainly be the rational thing for God to

do—but we're none of us God nor shall we ever understand all His ways. If we did, either He would cease to be God, or we would share His Lordship—neither of which is a likely contingency.

In this case I suggested that healing prayer for the child should be accompanied by prayers for the conversion of the parents; and that these prayers should *not* take the form of an attempt to bribe God by saying: "Heal Ann and her parents will come to You"; but to pray rather that God's way be opened for them, and His will done in their child.

This incident took place about a year ago. Since that time the parents have *themselves* begun to take their daughter to healing services—and it is obvious to those who know them that His way is being slowly but surely opened to them, and His will being fulfilled in the child. She is not as yet wholly well, but appears to be on the way to complete recovery.

For those whose loved ones are ill, positive intercessory prayer is of vital importance—and it is well to ask prayer not only for the patient's recovery, but also the spiritual strength of the family that they may prove better channels for His healing power. No matter how strong one's faith, the closer the one who is sick, the more difficult the situation tends to be. Our fear, however, which is almost inevitable, should never prevent our praying for those we love, for love is stronger than fear. Nor should we, I think, in our determination to pray the affirmative prayer of faith, feel guilty or ashamed if all we can at times muster is: "Christ have mercy upon us." I think we should not underestimate this prayer, for it is one He never fails to hear—and in my experience, to honor.

The young son of a woman who firmly believed in the healing Christ, was stricken with spinal meningitis. The medical prognosis was negative. Distraught and fearful, the mother called a friend experienced in prayer and asked her help. They agreed upon a certain hour at which time the *friend* would pray for healing, while the *mother* laid hands upon her son

This procedure was repeated three different times, and the child made an unprecedentedly rapid and complete recovery. The doctor in charge called it a miracle.

Dr. Alexis Carrel, distinguished surgeon and Nobel Prize winner, says: "Prayer has sometimes, so to speak, an explosive effect. Patients have been cured almost instantaneously of lupus of the face, cancer, kidney troubles, ulcers, tuberculosis of the lungs, of the bones or peritoneum."

The physical cures resulting from intercessory prayer are, in fact, no more dynamic than the spiritual ones, but they are more dramatic, and the *tangible* results of prayer are more readily computable in physical healing than in other areas. Here we are able to correlate the healing with the precise time of prayer, which gives us the clear-cut evidence of cause and effect.

Take the case of a woman, according to her doctors dying of cancer, who had been in a coma for forty-eight hours. Her husband asked for prayer, which was subsequently offered at 10 A.M. while he knelt, also in prayer, at her bedside. At 10:35 A.M. the woman opened her eyes, raised herself on her elbow, and said to her husband: "Honey, I'm starved! Did I sleep through breakfast?" She left the hospital ten days later. This was five years ago, and she has had no return of symptoms.

From personal experience I know that one is greatly helped by prayer whether or not the individual knows he is being prayed for. From observation, I know that even the unbeliever can receive healing through the prayers of the believer. But as a general rule, the patient should not only know (or if he is unconscious, as in the case previously mentioned, a close relative should know) but cooperate if he is able, by praying at the same time as the intercessory prayer is being offered.

It is common practice in the healing ministry to receive the laying on of hands, not only for ourselves, but on behalf of those for whom our prayers are offered. We do this for a dual purpose: as an implementation of our prayers; and the means whereby we may receive an increase of the Holy Spirit in our own lives—for the more we ourselves have of Him, the more effective our prayers, and the more efficaciously we may serve as instruments of His healing.

Whenever I receive the laying on of hands with special intention for someone, I ask that the patient be in prayer at the same time. Conversely, I have on my prayer list a number of people in other cities who attend healing services where they live. I am in prayer for them at home at the same hour that they are receiving the healing rites.

There is a constant tendency, even among those of us who know best its power, to disparage prayer, by saying in a hopeless tone of voice when told of serious illness or other disaster: "Well, all we can do now is pray." It may be *all* we can do, but at the same time, it is *everything*. I think that we should not hesitate to ask the prayers of others when we feel the need, but never should we ask *casually*—for real prayer is not a pink tea or a kafe klatche.

Many people who call me say apologetically: "I know you're busy, and I hate to ask anything more of you, but would you *mind* praying for so and so?"

Mind? It seems to me that to pray for others is quite possibly the greatest privilege that any of us can ever know. That through our prayers we may be instrumental in releasing the power of God in the lives of others; that we can help in this way to fulfill *their* deepest need, gives a new and wonderful purpose to *our* lives. We receive far more than it lies in our power to give, for our praying for others increases *our* sensitivity and receptivity to prayer, which in turn brings us always closer to the God we worship. "And the Lord turned the captivity of Job, when he prayed for his friends" (Job 42:10).

Chapter 14

the fellowship of the concerned

In union there is strength—and prayer is no exception. The prayer group movement, a lay movement, has spread all over the world. There is scarcely a country, including the communist-dominated nations, where there cannot now be found small circles of men and women praying together, demonstrating the unchallengeable assertion that "As many as received Him, to them gave He power to become the sons of God" (John 1:12).

Here in the United States the movement is spreading like wildfire. We find these groups of the faithful functioning in such widely diverse places as the Nation's largest air base, a Church Home for elderly women, in San Quentin prison among the "lifers," and in a Roman Catholic home for unwed mothers. Serving as a powerful Christian witness of our government, are a number of dynamic groups in the U.S. House and Senate, plus others in the Capital comprised of high-ranking government officials and their wives.

In those churches which have prayer groups, every aspect of the Church's ministry is enriched and strengthened. I think it is no exaggeration to suggest that without the existence of such groups, there would be no healing ministry at all; for not only does a healing ministry without such prayer support inevitably seem to fail, but it is most often through the results of the prayers of the faithful that such a ministry is begun and empowered to proceed.

Take for example a church I visited two years ago. The pastor had not as yet instituted healing services, nor did he apparently have any plans for so doing in the immediate future.

"My people aren't ready for it yet," he had told me the night before I spoke. "The truth is, I'm not sure that I know enough about it."

The next day after my address several women came to me and asked that I prevail upon their minister to begin healing services. I explained that this was not my affair, and suggested that if they really wanted such services, they should first form a prayer group with their clergyman's consent.

Subsequently, five women of the parish arranged to meet weekly to study and to pray for the sick and for the establishment of a healing ministry in their church. Within a few months this group expanded to twelve, and the clergyman was so impressed with the spiritual power generated by the group, that within the year he inaugurated a healing ministry.

If corporate prayer were utilized to even a fraction of its potential, the course of history might well be altered. Through it, the power of God becomes a viable and unassailable force, frequently discernible by the unbeliever, who, no matter what he calls it, responds. As an agnostic psychologist, at my instigation reluctantly present in a church where hundreds prayed in faith for the sick, remarked: "I am not prepared to call what I feel here, God—but neither will I argue that a force of some kind is being released."

"Where two or three are gathered together in My Name, there am I in the midst of them," said Our Lord (Matt. 18:20); and anyone who has felt the power of corporate prayer knows how true this is.

I have felt this power in a living room, where five people prayed together for the restoration of a broken marriage.

I have felt it in a parish hall, where group prayer was offered for the mending of international relationships.

I have felt it in a church, lit by the light of Christ, as many knelt in prayer for the recovery of a sick child. And most recently I felt it in a church in the midwest where I had gone to speak.

When I arrived that afternoon, I was told that the Roman Catholic husband of the church's caretaker had suffered a severe coronary attack the previous day. The medical prognosis was negative, and he had received the last rites of his Church at noon.

My audience that night was predominantly men, including a number of doctors of whom several were thought to be antagonistic to the healing ministry. Unusually sensitive to any hostility in an audience, I felt none that night either during the address or the question period which followed. Throughout, the Presence of God was so unmistakable, that as one man afterwards graphically expressed it: "If a dog had wandered in here tonight, his hackles would have risen."

At the conclusion of the program, the minister began the benediction—then abruptly halted, and visibly moved, said: "I feel so much power here I feel impelled to ask your prayers for someone who is, according to his doctors, dying." He told briefly of the patient's heart attack; the audience rose to its feet, and he proceeded to lead them in prayer for the sick man. The sense of the Presence seemed to increase, and as the prayers ended, the power seemed a palpable thing.

A week later I received a letter from the clergyman which said in part: "The night we prayed, the patient was awake and himself in prayer as he looked at the Crucifix on the wall of his hospital room. He suddenly became aware of the presence of a *second* person in the room, and heard the words: 'You will live, and you are saved by prayer. But not your own.' "

The patient is now well, and the doctors say that "a power beyond the skill of any physician" is responsible for his recovery.

My personal experience has been largely with prayer groups

directly related to the healing ministry; but in the over-all sense, *all* prayer groups are healing prayer groups, petitioning that the healing Christ touch every area of our lives and of the world. Their universal purpose is that outlined by Bishop Pardue: to pray more effectively; to generate power for the needs of others; to uplift and strengthen the faith of one another, and above all and in all these things, to glorify God.

No matter how familiar I become with the staggering power of prayer, I still find myself amazed at its actual, concrete force. This has been brought home to me again and again, not only in vitally important matters, but in inconsequential ones, such as when I am speaking. I rarely know ahead of time if any groups are praying for me, but the moment I start to talk, I know beyond the shadow of a doubt. Last week, for instance, my plane had arrived just in time for the address, and when I began I had no idea whether that particular church had any prayer groups within it. I soon found out, for as soon as I opened my mouth I felt, what was to me, the terrifying lack of prayer support. It was all I could do to finish.

A few months ago I witnessed a thrilling and not unusual example of the power of group prayer.

It was in the south during a three-day healing mission. On the first night a young woman came to me and told me that her husband had been for some time in a mental institution, suffering from schizophrenia. He was to be released for a trial weekend the following week. "But I'm going to try to get him out to come to this mission," she said. "I know how much good it will do him."

I must confess that I was frankly dubious. It seemed unwise to bring a still-ill mental patient, one of whose symptoms was a violent and emotional antipathy to religion, to a healing mission on his first day out of the hospital.

Before going to the church the next night, I spoke to one of the prayer group members and asked that if he should come, they sit together as a group directly behind him, holding him, not me, in prayer.

When I began my address I saw him sitting with his wife directly under the pulpit. In the middle of my talk I saw him rise and begin to come towards me. My eyes caught those of the group leader, and I knew they would go into prayer instantly. I watched the man closely, and what I saw was almost uncanny. It was as if an unseen force had stopped him in his tracks and was now pushing him onto his knees. He was to kneel for the remainder of a long service. Throughout, the Presence of God was so abundant in that church that had an atom bomb exploded in our midst, I think no one would have been harmed.

He came to me afterwards, started to speak but couldn't, as the tears streamed down his face. No words were necessary. I knew what he wanted to say. He returned the following night, sat quietly, and went up to the altar rail for the laying on of hands. I learned later that when he returned to the mental hospital after his trial two days at home, the doctors found him inexplicably improved. He was permanently released a short time later, and is now working at a full-time job. He is also an active and dedicated worker in his church.

How any particular healing group functions must be determined by the desire of its members and the environment which surrounds them. In many churches with healing ministries, a good proportion of the prayer group attends each service. The presence and prayers of expectant believers spiritually strengthen the officiating clergyman and are of great benefit to those at the service with perhaps a less developed faith, who are seeking healing. In some churches it is customary when there is a special and urgent need, to notify the prayer band, which then attends the service en masse, receiving the laying on of hands with special intention for the critically-ill person.

Take the case of a man with lung cancer. A member of the

prayer group was notified one night that the patient was not expected to live another twenty-four hours. Other members of the group were immediately informed, and within an hour the "prayer power" was turned on.

A special healing service was held by the rector the next morning at 8 A.M., at which time each member of the prayer group received the laying on of hands. At 9 A.M. the patient rallied, and his improvement continued. He went back to work within the month, and for three years every laboratory test has been negative.

Many prayer groups are formed by members of the International Order of St. Luke the Physician, founded by Episcopal clergyman John Gaynor Banks in 1947. Comprised of clergy and laity who feel impelled to make the ministry of healing a regular part of their vocation, the Order's interdenominational membership includes doctors, psychologists and registered nurses.

Since the Order began its work in Europe, psychiatrists there have been greatly impressed by its beneficial effects upon their patients. Recent statistics issued by the world-renowned University Hospital for Mental Diseases in Vienna, have resulted in an increasing number of psychiatrists who not only enlist the aid of these intercessory prayer bands, but are forming prayer groups among themselves to pray for their patients.

This same practice is now beginning to occur in the United States. Those doctors who are familiar with the healing ministry and therefore sympathetic to it, ask the cooperation of prayer groups. When a patient is seriously ill, the doctor asks for intercessory prayer; and in some instances, requests members of the prayer group to pray at the bedside of a patient. Not long ago, for example, a teen-age boy involved in an automobile accident, lay crushed and apparently dying in a large city hospital. Four members of a prayer group were called, and prayed together at his bedside for over two hours. The boy recovered, to the astonishment of all but one doctor—the one who had contacted the prayer group—who said: "When you made your prognosis you forgot to take into account the power of prayer."

In an Ohio city, a doctor and his wife, both members of the OSL, are responsible for a true spiritual revival which has touched not only many lives, but revitalized a number of churches in that area. Under the leadership of this couple, numerous prayer groups comprised of both men and women have been organized, and a healing ministry instituted in the city's largest church.

It was a wonderful and inspiring experience to visit there recently: to learn of the college students who had formed prayer bands; to meet the young married couples to whom God was first and prayer the top priority in their lives; to talk with the lawyers and engineers and doctors who are members of prayer groups, meeting weekly at noon in one of their offices, and to hear them say, faces alight: "I'd rather miss any other meeting on my calendar than the prayer-group meeting"; to meet a recent widow left with two young children, whose desire to impart to others her love of God, superseded her own grief; to know the alcoholic, who through group prayer in her behalf had found God, and in the finding had lost her desire and her need to drink; to see a couple who had lost a child, marvellously sustained by the power of God released through intercessory prayer; to meet the parents of a crippled child, who imbued everyone they met with a portion of their faith in and knowledge of, the mercy of God.

These are some of the works, and the fruits of the fellowship of the concerned, to whom religion is a vital, dynamic seven-day-a-week proposition.

As the most effective movements seem to be interdenominational—such as Unity, which has taught and proved to countless thousands the power of prayer—so have I noted that generally the most effective prayer groups are those which include members of different churches. It is often as an Episcopalian observed: "For several years we have struggled along with a purely Episcopal group. A few months ago we included a Baptist, a Methodist and a Presbyterian, and the group has assumed a new vitality. We have now had manifested startling evidence of the healing Christ." Perhaps this is because we have in these mixed groups an infinitesimal approximation of the power of the Church Universal.

I recently heard a clergyman refer to prayer-group work as a "vocation," and I recalled the words of St. Paul: "I therefore beseech you that ye walk worthy of the vocation wherewith ye are called" (Eph. 4:1).

In order to "walk worthy," I believe there must be a proper balance struck between prayer groups and the sacramental life of the Church. We all need the stabilizing influence of the Church if we are to avert those dangers which are inherent in any lay religious work—the danger of pride: "Our prayers are better than any others." The danger of feeling ourselves members of the spiritual elite, who alone know "how" to pray; the danger of spiritual arrogance, which is surely greater than any other arrogance on earth except that of ignorance; the danger of an ostentatious religiosity, which more often repels than converts. *Responsibility* I believe a group *must* feel, but never self-esteem, for nothing accomplished through intercessory prayer is done by any human being, or in any way involves personal merit.

Take the case of a doctor desperately ill with cancer of the liver. "If only I could *really* believe in God," he said to the chaplain, "I could die happy."

The chaplain enlisted the aid of a prayer group. "Pray for physical healing," he said, "but above all pray for a healing of the spirit so that this man may know God."

After several weeks of prayer the physician's condition began to improve. Then he said to the chaplain: "Last night I was able to pray for the first time since I was a child. I felt the undeniable Presence. Now I don't care what happens."

This was four years ago. He has long since resumed his practice, apparently in perfect health. This is the power of God—not the superiority of any one praying group.

Not long ago a hard-working church member voiced her interest in organizing a prayer group. "But the trouble is," she ended, "I haven't time—nor has anyone else I know."

E. Stanley Jones comments that if a church loses its power to convert, it has lost its right to be called Christian. Perhaps we who are so busy with our church bazaars and teas that we haven't time to pray, are losing our right to be numbered among the faithful. I do not question the worthiness of church activities, performed in His Name; I only wonder if we should not pause more frequently in our feverish "busy-ness" to remind ourselves that Jesus was not crucified for bigger and better bake sales.

The luncheon given for Russian Premier Khrushchev in Pittsburgh in 1959, was attended by 300 prominent Pittsburghers, among them Bishop Pardue and several members of local prayer groups. At one table sat a group leader flanked on one side by the Russian Minister of Agriculture, who spoke no English, and on the other by Mr. Fomin of the Russian State Department, who spoke the language brokenly.

As they talked she glanced around the room, and as if propelled in his direction, her eyes met those of the Bishop, and a second later, the eyes of two members of her prayer group in another portion of the room. She prayed silently as she knew the others were doing, and suddenly, for no apparent reason, there fell a curious hush over the dining room.

Mr. Fomin looked startled and said: "What has happened? I have a strange feeling. In here it seems now like a church."

Just then the minister who was to give the invocation stood up.

"Who's he?" asked Mr. Fomin, "and what is he going to do?"

"He's going to give the invocation," replied my friend.

"What's that?" queried the Russian, but before a reply was possible the minister began to pray, and everyone, including the Russians, bowed their heads. When it was over, Mr. Fomin said: "This has not happened since we have been in the United States. Do you do this only in Pittsburgh?"

My friend explained that many large meetings customarily begin with an invocation and end with a benediction. "Then why haven't they done this in other places where we've been?" asked the Russian. "I don't know why, but this has made me feel very good."

Here we see in action the potential power of prayer. This is why those of us who believe in prayer, believe that through it, the world can be saved.

We do not *understand* the power of corporate prayer; or why receiving the laying on of hands on behalf of others is effective; or why it is usually important that the person for whom intercessory prayer is offered should pray simultaneously, wherever he may be. We only know that experience has proved again and again that these things are so.

We also know that through the fellowship of the concerned, who believe that God loves and cares, His healing light is being released upon a sick and suffering world; that these groups of devout men and women, quietly and unobtrusively demonstrating His promised power, are His witnesses "unto the uttermost parts of the earth" (Acts 1:8).

Chapter 15

"as many as touched him were made whole"

Mark 6:56

Your healing does not depend upon personally attending healing services, for God is not confined to our churches although He should be centered there.

Thousands have been marvellously healed in their own homes through prayer. Many have been healed while they listened to religious programs on radio or television, as was a woman suffering from a ruptured disc who was instantly cured as the Word of God came to her over the air waves. Others, like a man healed of diabetes, have received God's power by merely *reading* about the healing Christ.

I think that few of us would disagree with Billy Sunday's trenchant remark: "Going to church doesn't make you a Christian any more than going to a garage makes you an automobile!" The Church, in itself, can't save our souls, but it is the agency through which we may be saved. Obviously we can't be theologized into salvation, because our salvation depends on our personal relationship with God. But at the same time, I believe that this relationship can come to full fruition only through the Church; for it is the Church and not the individual which is the extension of the Incarnation.

Not long ago I heard a man remark: "I practice my own private Christianity, and I don't need any church to help me do it. I'll wager that sitting here on my own porch overlooking the vastness of the sea, I'm more conscious of God than you people sitting in church on Sunday morning."

It is true that all believers are conscious of God as we view the magnificence of His creation; but to contemplate His handiwork and to acknowledge His Authorship is neither to experience nor to possess Him.

"Any man who has genuine contact with Christ, has this life" (1 John 5:12—Phillips). Conceding as I must that the means of grace include not only prayer and the Word but also the Sacraments, to neglect any of these is, in my opinion, to have a less than complete contact with Him—and therefore to deprive ourselves of the fullness of His power.

Actually there is no such thing as "private" Christianity, for according to Our Lord it is a communal affair. "When *two* or *three* are gathered together in My Name," He said, "there am I in the midst of them" (Mark 18:20).

"When ye pray," He said, "say 'Our Father which art in Heaven' " (Luke 11:2); not *my* Father. And throughout the Gospels we see the Faith laid down by Jesus to a fellowship; its members spiritually linked in His Mystical Body, and spiritually nourished there by His Incarnate Life.

However, regardless of your theological convictions, the healing Church has distinctly practical advantages you can't afford to overlook. The very nature of the healing services heightens our expectancy; while our faith is galvanized into new vitality by the faith of those who surround us.

The experience of a woman suffering from glaucoma, is typical. "I *know* that God heals," she said some months ago, "but somehow it seems harder to believe His healing for oneself than for others. The more I pray the less conviction I seem to have that God will heal *me*." Her church did not have healing services, so I suggested that she attend those of a nearby church of another denomination. A few weeks later she reported: "The people in that church *expect* something wonderful to happen, and it always does, whether or not they are physically healed. Their faith is an almost palpable thing, and it's contagious. All during the week now I pray with a new certainty that His healing is for *all* of us. Through the healing services my faith is continually replenished and sustained, and I'm beginning to understand what this ministry really means. My doctor was astonished at the improvement in my eyes yesterday."

But the healing Church is never solely a complement—an adjunct—to our private devotions; nor are the sacramental healing rites ever a substitute for personal prayer, as one woman seemed to think when she said, with obvious relief: "Thank goodness my church has instituted healing services. Now I can let up on prayer at home!"

The healing rites are not magical short cuts to God. It is not Unction, but our faith which brings us to Him; and it is not the laying on of hands, but prayer, on which our relationship with God depends. Yet these rites, as with all the Sacraments, when received with prayer and in faith, purvey grace to an extraordinary degree.

It is through this grace that the woman mentioned learned to pray. Her first *real* prayer, as was mine, was silently voiced at the altar rail where, touched by the Holy Spirit, she began to hunger for the Kingdom.

She learned there that real prayer is not an endless supplication. It is God's ordained method by which we can communicate with Him—and more important, the means by which He communicates with us. Through it, His power is released in our lives; and by it, His will is fulfilled on earth.

Anyone who prays knows that prayer is the greatest spiritual *and* physical reviver we have at our disposal, and yet many of us, myself included, are afflicted from time to time with what can best be described as a profound spiritual exhaustion. This most often occurs after we have been praying for a long time for someone close to us. I have learned that this is never the result of praying too *much,* but in my case at least, of not praying *well* enough; of praying with too much intensity; of failing to *relinquish* the one for whom we pray; of perhaps subconsciously trying to twist God to *our* purposes, instead of praying that He use us for *His.*

Then there are times which grow less frequent as we learn to pray, when we are strung to so high a pitch of tension that our prayers cease to be a means of communication with God, but become instead tension-propelled assaults upon Him. Our frenetic attempts to reach Him then result not in more strength but in complete depletion.

At these times a quiet church becomes a sanctuary where, immersed in God, our nerves are calmed and our minds rested. But the healing Church provides infinitely more than asylum. It is the fountainhead of the Holy Spirit, where we may hold out our cup of need, confident that it will be filled—the only limit to its capacity our own ability to receive.

"I can do all things through Christ which strengtheneth me. (Phil. 4:13) These words assume a new and power-charged reality, as at the altars of the healing Church we encounter the living God; and through the healing Sacraments touch the Hem of His Garment. It is this direct contact with Him which many of us need for complete healing.

Take the case of a man who suffered a severe coronary. His wife immediately gave his name to several prayer groups; and his doctor vouchsafed that in his opinion, it was the power released through prayer which saved the man's life. His heart, however, was so severely damaged that he was unable to resume work. It was a prayer-group member who suggested that he attend healing services, undergirded with group prayer.

"I've prayed and gone to church all my life," the erstwhile patient was to say, "but it was at these services that I first really *knew* that Christ lived. I actually felt His touch at the altar rail."

As a corollary to this knowledge, came the complete healing, verified by electrocardiogram. This man is now back at work. His physical healing was dramatic, but no more so than his spiritual transformation.

Active participation in the healing ministry, whether you pray for others or seek healing for yourself, can change your life as it has thousands of others, including my own. Exactly how this comes about, I don't pretend to know. Much in human life is real—evil, suffering, love—without being rationally comprehensible: and so it is with the healing power of God, which is a truth whose validity does not depend upon our comprehension of it. However, this I *do* know, not only from personal experience, but from widespread observation: it is the overwhelming sense of Our Lord's nearness at healing services; the magnification of His Presence in the healing Church, which can and will transform your life. This is a phenomenon which has been noted by so many who are neither mystics nor fanatics that I think it is no longer open to question.

Through the healing Church an alcoholic permanently loses all desire for alcohol; a narcotic addict goes off heroin with no withdrawal symptoms; a man is healed in three weeks of an anxiety neurosis of five-years' duration; a juvenile delinquent accepts Christ; and those many of us who suffer only from the ordinary frustrations and tensions of everyday living, learn for the first time in our lives what the "peace that passeth all understanding" really means.

"I am come that they might have life, and that they might have it more abundantly," He said (John 10:10). To realize this life in all its fullness, avail yourself, whether you are sick or well, of *all* the wonderful means God has given us: prayer, repentance and absolution, Holy Communion, and if you are able, attend healing services regularly. But in all these things, make sure that your primary goal is God; for if you seek healing instead of Him, you commit a heresy which will in all likelihood deny you both.

If you are housebound, let the Church come to you, as it did in the case of a young woman suffering from cancer of the brain, and blind as a result. She was in the prayers of many, but she said to me: "If *only* I could be sure that God lives."

When her mother called me one night in desperation, I suggested that she make arrangements to have the girl anointed.

"When the clergyman came, Mary was unconscious," her mother told me later, "but when he made the Sign of the Cross on her forehead, she opened her eyes, smiled, and said three words: 'Now I know.' "

The patient has now been anointed three times. It is too soon to claim a physical healing, but her condition has steadily improved, and she has regained her sight. Spiritually, she is now whole.

A clergyman, dissatisfied with his ministry of healing, questioned me concerning fasting in relation to healing. "I've never asked my congregation to fast before the healing service," he said. "Do you think I should?"

I could not possibly overemphasize what I believe to be the importance of this. Not only is fasting an act of faith, however small, a sacrificial act, however slight, but by quickening the spirit it inestimably increases our receptivity to the power of God. In my experience it has proved a virtually indispensable condition of healing.

About two weeks after our discussion, the clergyman called me. "I suggested," he said, "but did not demand, that my people fast before the service. Frankly I was astonished that they all acted on my suggestion. Never in my entire ministry have I witnessed such a tremendous outpouring of the Holy Spirit as at that service."

This is always the case when a group of fasting, praying people gather together, united by the desire to know their Lord.

There is nothing new about fasting. For centuries it has

gone hand-in-hand with prayer, but only lately, and largely in association with the healing ministry, does there seem to be a widespread awakening to its spiritual value. Just within the past year I have received innumerable queries, most of which ask: "How long should one go without food; under what circumstances; what do *you* do?"

On the basis of what I have seen and experienced, I would strongly urge everyone, unless medically advised to the contrary, to fast before a healing service. If it is in the morning, do without breakfast. If in the evening, omit dinner. The length of the fast must depend upon the individual; his state of health, and his ability to go without food without suffering seriously adverse effects.

Speaking strictly for myself: as part of the discipline of the healing ministry, I fast routinely one day a week—and a second day if there is an extremely urgent need for healing—eating nothing all day until dinner at night. This doesn't hurt my health, but it might well harm others and therefore can't be recommended as general practice. But I do recommend the theory behind it, whether you seek healing for yourself or pray for the healing of others. I have found this weekly fast to be of great value, but if it proves deleterious to your health, don't do it. Your fast is not a self-inflicted penalty for sin, but a sacrifice, freely offered, for love. Remember that even St. Francis towards the end of his life began to wonder if his long abuse of his body had not constituted sin. Even if you, like some, suffer only a severe headache when you go without food, don't do it. Your mind will be so occupied with how badly you feel that you will miss the point of the fast—which is to remind you of God—not of the aspirin bottle! If you can manage only to curtail your usual intake of food, you will gain in receptivity, and God will honor your intention. But whatever the discipline you impose upon yourself, don't publicize it: "That thou appear not unto men to fast, but unto thy Father which is in secret" (Matt. 6:18).

"But I've been fasting and going to healing services for months," a woman protested, "and while I have been greatly helped spiritually, my physical condition is no better. Should I stop praying for healing?"

Probably the best answer to this question lies in the case of a man brought to my attention only last week. He has suffered for seven years from what his doctors termed irreversible blindness, due to a severed optic nerve. Throughout this time he has prayed for healing, and only now has begun to receive his sight.

The vast majority of healings todays are gradual, probably due to the wall of unbelief which still surrounds us, regardless of our personal convictions. In view of the many remarkable but delayed healings which occur, my advice must always be to continue to pray once each day; then command yourself or the one for whom you pray, to God, confident that "through faith and patience you shall inherit the promises of Our Lord" (Heb. 6:12).

While you await your healing, abide in the love of God, resting in the promise: "Come unto me, and I will answer thee, and show thee great and mighty things which thou knowest not" (Jer. 33:3). Offer your sickness to Him, and He will sanctify it. Thus it will become a sacrifice offered to His glory, rather than the sterile, purposeless thing it now appears to be. But never forget that your sickness of itself is not of God but of the enemy. Continue to fight it, knowing that each blow you strike brings you closer to Him, because you are fighting, in His Name, for the fulfillment of His ultimate will.

A man healed of lung cancer, reports: "I felt a searing heat across my chest." A woman cured of a congenital deformity, states: "It felt like a current of electricity going through my body from head to toe." However, these physical sensations, although they often accompany healing, are not necessarily indicative of it. To *expect* them as inevitable signs of healing, can often block God's power, as in the case of a woman who said with discouragement: "I guess I'm not going to be healed, because I've never felt either heat or electricity when I received the laying on of hands."

In talking with her it became obvious that her anxiety had of itself created a barrier. When she understood that most healings came quietly, she relaxed her concern, and His healing power flowed through her.

A more common, although by no means universal indication of healing, is a temporary intensification of symptoms. The experience of a man healed of a brain tumor, is fairly typical.

Suffering from excruciating headaches, he had attended healing services for two months. Then one day during the laying on of hands: he suddenly felt God so close he wouldn't have been surprised to hear Him speak. At that moment he knew he was healed."

He thanked God, and held hard to his belief that he had received healing, although his pain increased to the point where he was obliged to leave the service. In agony for two days, the pain gradually diminished, until by the end of the third day he was pain-free. An encephlogram a week later confirmed the healing.

The more deeply I have become involved in the healing ministry, the more acutely aware I have become that God's inscrutable majesty and awesome power are never far removed from His redeeming love and infinite mercy. I have at last learned that if we would know Him and receive His power, we must accept Him strictly on *His* terms, however difficult or even unpalatable they may seem to us—and not ours.

We are taught that God does not coerce us; that we have free will to accept or reject Him, and of course this is true. Yet *having* accepted Him, His demand for our lives in their entirety might be construed as a form of coercion. Once having made our commitment, we are indeed, as St. Paul says.

His prisoners (Eph. 4:1); and that our shackles are love makes them but the more binding. Once having made our act of faith; once having surrendered ourselves to Him, we are forever His.

In my own life I have discovered the implacable truth in His words: "To whom much is given, of him will be much required" (Luke 12:48 RSV). I have come to believe that He demands of us a commitment in accordance with our knowledge of Him. If our commitment is already great, so is our responsibility; and the smallest deviation, overlooked in the less committed, can have disastrous consequences; for "If we sin deliberately after receiving knowledge of the truth, there no longer remains a sacrifice for sins, but a fearful prospect of judgment" (Heb. 10:26).

I have found that these words constitute not a threat, but a statement of fact. Once having known His light we cannot, by a deliberate act of will, turn from it, however slightly, without engendering a soul-destroying conflict within ourselves. In order to escape the here and now consequences of our rebellion, we turn again to God—and in this sense He has forced us back to an unqualified commitment to Himself. But this is not "coercion." It is rather another evidence of His supreme mercy; that in taking us back again and again, we may avert His final judgment.

"Among all the attributes of God, although they are all equal, mercy shines with even more brilliance than justice" (Cervantes). We who have so often experienced it, know this to be true; as we know that above all and in all and through all, is the love of God. This is the sovereignty by which He rules; the power by which we are at once enslaved and set free. Before it we are helpless; through it we are incredibly empowered; without it we cannot live, nor would we want to.

The healing ministry has opened thousands of unreceptive hearts to His mercy, as it has mine. It has demonstrated to countless unbelieving minds, as to my own, the dynamic reality of His love.

A woman in Connecticut lies dying of cancer, and says: "I am only afraid of the pain, for I don't stand pain well." The love of God overcomes her fear, and she is healed.

A man in Colorado, in coma with uremia, receives Unction. The love of God penetrates his subconscious, and he is made whole.

A widow in California, suffering an agony of loneliness, experiences Our Lord at the altar rail. The love of God assuages her grief, and she finds peace.

"We would see Jesus" (John 12:21)? He stands now revealed with unparalleled clarity and unprecedented power, in the healing Church. He has indeed "visited and redeemed His people" (Luke 1:65). For the love of God and in His Name, let us dare to claim our redemption in all its fullness.

Chapter 16

the greatest of all healing services
"that we may worthily receive"

BCP, p. 81

There is no one method alone by which we can find the living, healing Christ. But for each of us there is a "best" way, which according to the dictates of our hearts and consciences we are compelled to follow as if it were the "only" way.

All Christians must live by the creeds, but we who are members of a liturgical church must live also by the Sacraments; which is to say that for us there is in the Sacraments a very real and wonderful power. Without them, we are, as the Eastern Orthodox Church expresses it, "helpless, hopeless and lifeless."

While I fully recognize that God is not bound by the Sacraments, I must frankly confess that I am. Therefore, although for me there is neither full life nor complete healing outside of them, I realize that this obviously does not hold true for many thousands of others.

But regardless of church affiliation or sacramental emphasis, the immeasurably great healing power inherent in Holy Communion cannot be denied. It can be the greatest Sacrament of healing Our Lord has given us when we grasp in even the smallest measure, its meaning and significance.

I am quite aware that many people comprehend and have

experienced the power latent in the Eucharist without benefit of the healing ministry; but for me and for many, one of the most thrilling results of this ministry has been to illumine in almost incredible fashion, the great Sacrament instituted by Our Lord.

For me this illumination has not come about suddenly. It is as if the healing ministry had first lit a small candle, shedding just enough light with its tiny point of flame, to make discernible a blurred outline of some of the great truths inherent in the Sacrament, while others still remained hidden in the shadows. But gradually the light from this one candle has grown brighter and brighter until at last it has exploded into the brilliance of many suns, penetrating every corner of the darkness, exposing truths I never dreamed existed. While the *full* meaning of this Sacrament must remain always shrouded in mystery, enough has been revealed to forever change my life.

I see now in Holy Communion, not only the meaning but the means of salvation; the difference between *sensing* the Presence as we do through prayer and meditation, and *experiencing* God; the difference between an awareness of Him, however intense, and the living God Himself; the difference between acknowledging the *fact* of our redemption, and actually knowing the redemptive *power*.

This communion of the Body and Blood of Christ is many things: It is a continual pledge—the supreme expression of His love "to our great and endless comfort" (BCP, p. 86).

It is a re-enactment of His Self-offering; a re-presentation of His Sacrifice. It is the memorial Christ commanded us to make; the perpetual remembrance of His Passion; a restatement of the four great parts of His redemptive work: the Incarnation, Crucifixion, Resurrection and Ascension. It is *our* sacrifice of praise and thanksgiving for the "innumerable benefits procured unto us by the same" (BCP, p. 81).

It is these things and much more, but above all it is the means by which His love is actualized *for* us and activated *in* us; the means by which we can receive not only His grace, but the living Christ Himself.

"But," someone remarked to me a short while ago in a definitely belligerent tone, "Our Lord clearly said, 'This do in remembrance of me.' Why, then, is the Lord's Supper anything more than just a memorial to Him?"

My answer was two-fold: first, the Greek wording for "do this in remembrance," clearly implies not so much the *looking back* into a past event, as the bringing of the past into the present; second, and most important, read John 6: 48-63, which seems to me to state unequivocally exactly what Our Lord meant this Sacrament to be. I think that no one can read these verses and remain dubious as to His intention.

"I am the bread of life," He said, "and the bread that I will give is my flesh. Whoso eateth my flesh and drinketh my blood, hath eternal life" (John 6:48, 51).

This sharing of Our Lord's Body is more than communion. It is the fusion with Him which is the entire purpose of our being both now and forever.

I believe that in every human being there is a hunger for God however submerged; a yearning for grace, however stifled. Through this union with Him, our hunger is satisfied and our yearning stilled. We are more than cleansed by His redemptive grace. We are indwelt by the Redeemer Himself. How this mystery is brought about we cannot know. That it occurs, we cannot doubt. To the exact extent that we are able to receive Him, are we spiritually healed.

"Take, eat," He tells us. "This is my body which is given for you" (Matt. 26:26-28), And as we partake of the Body of Christ, not only our souls but our minds and bodies are marvellously strengthened.

"Drink ye all of this," He says, holding out the Cup, which is Himself, "for this is my blood of the new testament which is shed for you and for many, for the remission of sins." And as we partake of the Blood of Christ, we experience a transfusion which revitalizes every fiber of our beings. Pervaded by God, there is no room in us for disease.

In the early Church, when the wonder was new and faith was strong, the healing power inherent in the Eucharist was a well-established fact. Our Lord has not changed or diminished in either reality or power—only our faith in both has lessened. I am unalterably convinced that within this Sacrament today, as centuries ago, there is contained the total power of the Risen Christ. Emotionally I am so convinced because I, myself, have felt this power. Logically I am so convinced because according to my faith, I believe that Christ is of one Substance with the Father. In this Sacrament, according to His words, He offers Himself to man. Therefore, in receiving God, we are necessarily the recipients of all power. Rationally I am so convinced because I have seen the impact of this power on many lives.

I have known a man healed of tuberculosis after receiving Holy Communion at the altar rail. I have known a woman healed of stomach cancer after receiving the Sacrament in her hospital bed. I have watched ailing, self-interested, material-minded men and women become centers of His radiant life, saved in body, mind and spirit through the Body and Blood of Christ. And I have noted that these and scores of others like them, shared at least two things in common: their faith in the healing Christ, which had led them to new insights into the meaning of the Eucharist; and a belief that in this Sacrament of His Body and Blood they were contacting, however briefly, the supreme reality, which is God through Christ— from whom flows and in whom lies, all healing and all life.

I have come to believe that in Holy Communion healing is not only possible but *inevitable* for those who are able to receive Him—which is not so simple as it sounds, nor yet as difficult.

Why are not more of us changed either spiritually or physically after partaking of the Sacrament? Why, even by the time we leave the Church to go home, have most of us reverted to our old ways—seething with irritation because someone has parked too close and we can't get our car out; or boiling with resentment over something Mrs. Jones said on the church steps? Largely, I think, because although we may have been fleetingly brushed by His grace, we have been unable to receive *Him*. Impediments erected by our lack of understanding and of preparation and of faith, have prevented His indwelling.

As the Presence of Jesus is real whether or not human minds recognize it, so is His healing power residual in the Body and Blood whether or not we acknowledge it, and whether or not we are in a state whereby we can receive it. For the believer, everything depends on his own receptiveness. This I have learned can be dramatically increased by the grace of God, if we follow as best we can the adjurement of St. Paul to *carefully examine* ourselves before we "eat of that bread and drink of that cup" (1 Cor. 11:28). He tells us that if we fail to *prepare* ourselves we then eat and drink unworthily. He warns us that if we are impervious to the Presence of the Lord in His Church, we profane His Body and Blood, and "that is why many of you are weak and ill, and some have died" (1 Cor. 11:30).

Archaic words, you say? Just another obsolete scriptural teaching, obviously irrelevant and inapplicable to us today? I used to think so, but I now believe implicitly that its veracity is being proved thousands of times each year. As I have seen demonstrated, times without number, the validity of Our Lord's promises when claimed, so have I had manifested beyond any doubt the truth of St. Paul's teaching on the Eucharist. When it is disregarded I have seen in the Sacrament a vaguely uplifting, symbolic rite in honor, too often, of a largely hypothetical Saviour; a powerless commemoration of an Event long since obscured in legend. When it is heeded, I have known in the Sacrament the transforming reality of His Presence and the actuality of His redemptive power.

As St. Paul appears to associate "unworthiness" chiefly with lack of self-examination, the remedy becomes crystal clear.

Few of us today, as few nearly 2,000 years ago, partake of the Sacrament irreverently. Few would wittingly receive it sacrilegiously except in so far as our carelessness and indifference constitute an unintentional desecration. Yet how many of us receive it *unworthily* simply because of lack of preparation, whereby we "eat and drink damnation to ourselves" (1 Cor. 11:29); and incidentally deprive ourselves of the inestimable comfort and limitless power of His indwelling Self. I shudder now at *my* long indifference, when Holy Communion meant chiefly the unwelcome prolongation of the Sunday Service ("Don't tell me it's Communion Sunday *again!*"); and I mourn those lost years of self-privation when, in my carelessness I never took time out to prepare myself in any way for what now seems to me God's greatest gift to men.

The rationale of Paul's teaching never seemed more apparent than when it occurred to me that when we are preparing to receive guests in our home, we clean and polish and make sure that everything is in apple-pie order. Was the prospect of receiving Christ in our souls less important, then, than a buffet supper? Was trying to put our spiritual house in some semblance of order—as ready as we could make it for His coming—less worthy of our time and effort than a cocktail party?

The answer was self-evident: I could only wonder that it had taken me so long to pose the question.

The next step was the method of spiritual preparation.

Faith, love and repentance: these three are the foundation stones of the Christian Faith; the factors on which our healing depends; the hinges which swing wide the door of our heart to Christ. These, then, seem to me the vital areas of self-examination; the indispensable basis of our preparation.

The Invitation to Holy Communion offers us the simple framework on which we may build:

"Ye who do truly and earnestly repent you of your sins" (BCP, p. 75)

You may find it helpful, as have I, to make a mental listing of specific sins committed since the last Communion, there never being time to properly recall these in the General Confession. Obviously in doing this we are not telling God anything He doesn't already know, but it is a seemingly immutable Divine Law that He will not change our lives at the altar if we fail to freely acknowledge how badly they need changing.

Confess then your faults, and offer them to Christ that He may forgive them; that you may receive not only His absolving grace at the altar rail, but Himself, in a union which is destined to be broken again and again by our sin, but which our contrition unfailingly and continually restores.

"And are in love and charity with your neighbors."

Take a few minutes to meditate upon Our Lord's love, which we can mirror, however palely and imperfectly, in our love for others, "following the commandments of God." The love of Jesus for *you*, will be climaxed as He gives you again His Body and Blood, once given nearly 2,000 years ago, and re-offered spiritually, but none the less actually, each time you partake of this Holy Mystery.

"Draw near with faith."

Reflect now upon your faith—the determining factor of your receptiveness, as it is of your salvation. Without it, your act of contrition is a meaningless gesture; for how can you be sorry that your sin crucifies One whom you do not acknowledge? Without it, your meditation on love is a worthless waste of time; for how can you love One in whom you don't believe?

At least in the beginning, you might ask yourself some basic questions concerning the Sacrament you are soon to receive.

Do you *really* believe that this Sacrament was instituted by Our Lord—the unparalleled means by which we can continue to receive Him—or is there in the back of your mind the thought which I have heard expressed, that this is just another of the Church's inventions—a ritual-smothered gimmick?

Do you *really* believe that He is the Living Bread—and "if any man eat of this bread he shall live forever" (John 6:51)?

Ponder these things, then let "Lord, I believe; help thou mine unbelief" be your prayer as you consecrate yourself to Him.

However imperfect your self-examination, Christ will honor your efforts. He will enter your heart, and you will indeed be able to "take this Holy Sacrament to your comfort." This Sacrament which is the "medicine of all spiritual sickness; the means whereby not only the mind, but also the stricken bodies recover their former strength" (Thomas à Kempis).

Receive it fasting, as did the early Christians, that you may be spiritually sensitized to His Presence in all its fullness.

Receive it expectantly, as did the early Christians, so that you may know, perhaps for the first time, what St. Paul really meant when he said: "The Christ is a tremendous power within you" (2 Cor. 12:19 Phillips).

I have done these things—and I have felt within myself a fraction, however minute, of the indescribable power of the living Christ—and yet, as short a time as a year ago, there were periods when I considered myself "too busy" to receive the Sacrament at every opportunity that it was offered.

The last such period was when I was rushing to meet a deadline, and to take time off in the middle of the week seemed an expenditure of time I simply couldn't afford. As the weeks of long working hours went on, my fatigue increased and my output decreased until the prospect of meeting the deadline appeared hopeless. One night I decided that regardless of what it did to my work schedule, I would have to resume my custom of mid-week Communion, making up the time so spent by working late the preceding night. This I proceeded to do, and the result was instantaneous. Strengthened by the Holy Spirit, knowing again the resurgent power of the Christ, my fatigue vanished—and my work output increased far beyond my greatest expectations—and far beyond my own ability to achieve.

This is a very small and certainly unimportant thing, but it illustrates what not only I, but countless others have found to be true: the life-giving power in this Sacrament which enables so many of us to work and live far beyond our own capacities.

This is not to say that the living God is only present at the altar. He is as close to us as our hands and feet.

It is not to say that Christ dwells in us only when we receive the Sacrament. He abides with us every second of our lives.

Nor is it to say that the power of the Holy Spirit is confined to any church. It is released by faith, through prayer, wherever we may be. But in the Sacrament of Our Lord's Body and Blood, instituted by Him for our strengthening, our total restoration, that "our bodies and souls may be preserved unto everlasting life" (BCP, p. 83), there is an unprecedented intensification of His Presence, and an unexampled concentration of His power. Once having experienced Him in this particular way, to be deprived, is to be indeed, "helpless, hopeless and lifeless."

For a long time after I became interested in the healing ministry it used to concern me that the Holy Spirit invariably seemed to be more abundantly present during specific healing services than during the Eucharist. My concern was not lessened when I learned that this was not a reaction peculiar to me, but almost a universal one.

Why, I repeatedly asked myself, should this great Sacrament ordained by Our Lord Himself, and the central act of the Church, be so apparently devoid of power to all but a few? Could it be, I wondered, a question of expectancy; of faith; of concord? There was no doubt that in receiving the laying on of hands, everyone present was in complete unity of faith in the healing Christ—a faith unmarred by differences in theological concepts. To any such group of expectant believers, unified in a common faith, God makes Himself powerfully known. Then what was lacking, and why, in the Sacrament of Holy Communion? I finally concluded that among us who receive this Sacrament, there is *not* an unbroken unity of faith. Following the Protestant tradition of intense individualism, we tend to hold widely diverse views as to what we are doing, and what we should expect to happen, if anything, when we attend the Lord's Supper. Our common bond seems pietism, not faith; and the only area perhaps, in which we are in "one accord," would seem to be our general lack of expectancy.

The means Our Lord designated for sacramental use in Holy Communion are simple and universally available—bread and wine. Yet the concept of the Sacrament itself, seems to me far from simple. We echo the question asked twenty centuries ago: "How can this man give us His flesh to eat?" (John 6:32)—Asked then in bewilderment, it is small wonder that we continue to be puzzled today. But as is true in every area of the Faith, our confoundment does not nullify inherent truths; and what must always remain our lack of total apprehension, cannot impair the validity of His assertion: "He that eateth my flesh and drinketh my blood, dwelleth (abideth) in me and I in him" (John 6:56).

It took me a long time to learn to abide in *Him*, so that He might abide in me. It took me even longer to understand that unless I could receive Him, I could neither live nor give Him.

This indwelling of Christ in us and we in Him has seemed to me a complex thing. It is the personal relationship with Christ as Our Saviour which we have learned through the healing ministry, which has enabled many of us to better comprehend its meaning; a personal relationship which if not firmly established, can be obscured by the liturgy. Through the healing ministry, the danger that we will worship the *thing* and not the Person, has been eliminated. We know beyond the shadow of a doubt, Whom we seek, and why. We go to the altar to meet God. There we take Him to ourselves. We leave possessing Him.

Chapter 17

the greatest of all healing services
"with most humble and hearty thanks"

BCP, p. 86

I have spoken only of what we *receive* from the Sacrament of Holy Communion, and I must admit that for a long time this was my sole consideration. But I have found that as through the healing ministry we learn to know God better and to love Him more; as our gratitude becomes increasingly inexpressible, many of us reach the point when coupled with our ever-present desire to receive, is an overwhelming longing to *give*.

"This have I done for thee. What hast thou done for Me?" This question rings in our minds and echoes in our hearts, finally demanding answer.

The answer for me, and I know for many, has been found in the sacrificial Eucharist, which offers us a unique and wonderful means by which we can present to Him "ourselves, our souls and bodies, to be a reasonable, holy and living sacrifice, acceptable to God" (BCP, Rom. 12:1); the offering which is the best we know to give, and all we have.

While of course it is true that we may offer ourselves vicariously in every aspect of our daily lives; in all our human contacts ("For in as much as ye have done it unto the least of these, my brethren, ye have done it unto me"); in all that we do in His Name and strive to do to His glory, yet it is a

163

deep psychological need as well as a human desire to give a distinctly *personal* gift to the loved one—a gift specifically of and from ourselves. It is through this Holy Sacrament of mystical exchange, that we may give ourselves to Him, as Christ gives Himself to us.

In a sense, of course, we can only give to God that which He has first given us; that which is already His, as by Him we were created, and in Him we have our being. We can only try to offer Him those things which are most our own: our sin; our need; our weakness, and our entire will. The latter being the most difficult to relinquish, constitutes perhaps our only semblance of real sacrifice.

We pray with Loyola: "Take, O Lord, and receive my entire liberty, my memory, my understanding and my whole will. All that I am, all that I have, Thou hast given me, and I will give it back again to thee to be disposed of according to Thy good pleasure." In proportion to the completeness of our offering, does He return that which we have given—absolved, fulfilled, strengthened and sanctified—empowered to be more fully that which by His redemption we are meant to be.

Now we see in Holy Communion more than a Sacrament. It is also a consecration in which we are able to give Him back that which for some reason we know He wants—ourselves.

We see in it more than a channel for His grace. As God expressed Himself on earth through Jesus, so is this Sacrament the visible sign of His Real Presence, which is His legacy to all mankind forever.

"Except ye eat the flesh of the Son of man and drink his blood, ye have no life in you" (John 6:53).

The early Church implicitly believed these words. The twentieth-century Church is re-ascertaining their truth. It is interesting to note that there is a growing trend among many non-liturgical churches to place more emphasis on Holy Communion—

a trend accelerated by the healing ministry, where the power of the Sacraments is being re-discovered. Not only an increasing number of clergymen of all denominations, but also laymen, have become sensitive to what seems as true now as throughout the history of the Church: the unmistakable correlation between more frequent Communions and a corresponding enhancement of spiritual power in the Church.

Some months ago a member of a non-liturgical church stopped in to see me. Badly crippled by arthritis, and walking with the aid of two canes, he explained that he had been attending healing services at his church, but although spiritually helped, there had been no discernible improvement in his physical condition.

We talked for a while, and when it became clear that he had a good understanding of the healing ministry as far as he had gone, I asked him how long it had been since he had received Communion.

"Oh, I don't really remember," he said. "Probably about a year." He went on to explain that not only was the Sacrament offered infrequently at his church, but on the last two or three occasions when it had been offered, he hadn't felt well, and decided that it was not "worth the effort."

I could only tell him what I so firmly believe: that the days on which we feel the least well are the times when we need the Sacrament the most. How can we better receive healing than through the Body and Blood of Christ?

I suggested that he receive Communion the next time it was offered regardless of how he felt (provided, of course, that his doctor gave permission), and before receiving, that he prepare himself in the way I have outlined in the previous chapter.

A month later the man received the Sacrament, and walked out of the church using only one of his canes. He has continued to attend the healing services and receive Holy Communion whenever it is administered. He has long since abandoned the use of his second cane, and there is small evidence remaining of his formerly incapacitating disease.

The other day I met the Pastor of his church.

"You know," he said to me, "I never even faintly realized the extraordinary healing power in the Lord's Supper until a few months ago. Since then we have been preceding each healing service with Holy Communion, and the results have been truly astonishing."

The experience of this clergyman is far from unique, as is the case of a woman who wrote me some two years ago. At that time, reputedly dying of cancer, she had written in desperation to procure the name of a church in her vicinity which held healing services. Unfortunately there was none; but knowing that she belonged to a sacramental church, I suggested as I have so often before and since under similar circumstances, that she make the weekly celebration of the Eucharist at her church, *her* healing service. This she proceeded to do, and as in so many other like cases, her health dramatically improved.

No one who believes in the healing Christ need feel deprived of the incalculable benefits of the healing ministry—for although there are many churches which have not as yet instituted specific healing ministries, almost every Christian church offers Holy Communion. Make this, then, *your* healing service, partaking as often as you can. As your comprehension of this Sacrament grows; as by dint of God's grace and your own meticulous self-examination you receive it "worthily," your receptivity will increase until you are able to experience the power inherent in this greatest of all healing Sacraments.

I am convinced that if we only *faintly* apprehended what Holy Communion means; if we only *half* believed the words we say, we wouldn't so eagerly seize upon the pretext of inclement weather or slight indisposition to stay away. Rather would we be storming our churches to partake of the Body

and Blood of Our Lord. If we believed, it would be as Thomas
à Kempis has said: "Were the blessed Sacrament to be ministered in only one place and consecrated by one priest in the
world, with how great desire the people would run to that
place and that priest, that they might see there those heavenly
mysteries."

A year or so ago a woman deplored the fact that her church
offered Holy Communion only four times annually.

"I've been working with a healing prayer group," she said,
"and as my church has no healing ministry, I've been attending healing services elsewhere. I don't want to change my
church affiliation, but since I've been active in the healing
ministry I understand many things that were not clear before.
I feel a great need to receive Communion more frequently
than my church offers it."

Recently I saw this woman again, and discovered that
through the efforts of her group, her church is now celebrating
the Eucharist once a month.

"Before another year passes," she said, "we hope to have
Communion every week. It's strange, but as our interest in
spiritual healing has expanded, we seem better able to understand the meaning of the Sacrament. To more and more of
us it is becoming all-important."

For countless such people as well as myself, the ministry of
healing has resulted in a revelation which, however slight it
may be, has brought a knowledge which I think cannot be
imparted by any amount of teaching, however inspired; or any
number of sermons, however eloquent. If for no other reason
—if we had never witnessed a physical cure—the propensity of
the healing ministry to reveal spiritual truths in every area of
the faith; to induce a curious receptivity to these truths, would
more than justify its existence; proving beyond any dispute
that it is of God and according to His will.

I see now in Holy Communion, not just the heart of the
Church, but also the climax of our personal worship and the

apex of the healing ministry; the union, the welding together, the divine fusioning by which the fullest healing we can know on earth takes place—when Christ dwells in us and we in Him.

I see in this Sacrament the summation and the culmination of the Faith; comprising at once the justified means by Jesus, and the end, which is God.

I see focalized in Holy Communion, the epitome of our individual relationship with Christ.

When spiritually thirsty, I have found refreshment at His altar. "Come unto me all ye that travail and are heavy laden, and I will refresh you" (Matt. 11:28) are not empty words. The water that He gives me there becomes indeed a "spring of water welling up to eternal life" (John 4:14 RSV).

When spiritually desolate I have been most often reconciled with Him at the altar rail, where He "has brought me out of darkness into His own glorious light" (BCP, p. 77). In such moments of reconciliation, I have known the vindication for my existence.

In short, I have found in Holy Communion, not only the strength for my life, but life itself—for "hereby we know that He abideth in us, by the Spirit which He hath given us" (1 John 3:24).

"He that cometh to me shall never hunger; and he that believeth on me shall never thirst" (John 6:35).

This is the promise fulfilled beyond our deepest desire and most fervent hope, when at His altars we meet the Christ in a personal encounter which in its intensity, cannot, for many of us, be equalled by any other means. Face to face with the living God; invaded by the healing Christ; sanctified by the Holy Spirit, we know the full impact of His healing power. We stand on the threshold of the Kingdom where there "shall be no more death; neither sorrow nor crying; and neither shall there be any more pain" (Rev. 21:4).

Chapter 18

"in newness of life"

BCP

The vast majority are led to the healing ministry through their need for physical healing; but they come to learn that spiritual healing is not primarily the curing of the body by spiritual means, but the transfiguring of our lives when we encounter Jesus. They come to understand that the concept that God heals is more than a philosophy premised on desperate hope; and that the healing ministry is more than attending church services where they receive some mystic rites. It is a means of confrontation with the living God.

"I am the Way," He said—and for many of us the ministry of healing is the agency by which we come to better comprehend His Truth and more fully "experience His Life."

To live by faith in the healing Christ is to live by the *full* faith without which we are necessarily less than whole. It is to "put on the *whole* armour of God" (Eph. 6:13), that we may stand invulnerable and unafraid against evil.

Because the scope of this ministry is so broad that it touches every area of every individual's life; because each of us needs the healing Hand of Christ upon his life, spiritual healing is not alone for the physically sick. It is for all who long for a more intense awareness of the reality of God; for all who yearn for the assurance that He lives; for all who desire wholeness—

nervous, emotional and spiritual, as well as physical and mental.

To live by the healing ministry is to avert the too-common dilemma typified in a telephone call I received the other day.

"My brother is dying of an inoperable brain tumor," said the caller in distress. "The doctors don't want him to know how hopeless his condition is. He knows nothing of spiritual healing, and if I mention it to him now he will feel it a hopeless last resort. To be asked to cooperate in prayer would be completely meaningless to him, and to receive the healing rites would scare him to death."

Prayer is, of course, being offered now for this man, but he is being tragically deprived of the full healing power of God because of his unfamiliarity with the healing ministry.

"If any one does not take care of his own, and especially of his household, he has denied the faith" (1 Tim. 5:8). There are an increasing number of families for whom spiritual healing has become an accepted part of everyday living; who are well-versed in healing prayer, and to whom the sacramental healing rites are not a frightening ill-understood ritual, but familiar and infinitely comforting contacts with God.

A woman I know, for example, has brought up her two sons, aged thirteen and fourteen, with a knowledge of the healing Christ. A year ago, despite three vaccine "shots" they fell gravely ill—one with bulbar polio, and the other with only a slightly less virulent strain of the disease.

The mother immediately asked two local churches for prayer, and then called certain individuals whom she knew to be familiar with the power of prayer, taking care, even with these, not to indiscriminately reveal the nature of the ailment lest an aura of fear be created. She herself adamantly refused to consider the *results* of the sickness—death in the one case, and possible paralysis in the other—but concentrated her attack on the *disease*.

The boys, supported by prayer twenty-four hours a day, received the laying on of hands several times in the hospital. In spite of complications which the doctor predicted would be fatal for one of the boys, they were both discharged a short time later in perfect health.

The undaunted conviction of both children that God willed their recovery; that He could and would take over where medical knowledge ended; their ability to cooperate in prayer, were the factors which saved them, as one doctor frankly admitted.

When the two churches which had offered prayer for the polio victims were asked the following week to offer thanksgiving for their complete recovery, the members were flabbergasted at this demonstration of the healing power of God. Unfamiliar until now with the healing ministry, both these churches and others aware of what has happened, have been revivified by a new and vibrant faith.

It has been interesting to me to see the response of so many physically healthy young people to the ministry of healing. Through it, a religion which for most of them was simply another community project, has become a dynamic, power-filled faith. There are many now, like the college boy who developed mononucleosis. He asked at once for prayer, and was completely well in three days. Or like the twenty-year-old girl having her first baby, who was threatened with an unusually difficult birth. She asked for the laying on of hands, and the birth was quick and uneventful. "I never would have believed it possible," said the obstetrician. "You forgot the power of God," came the reply.

Many have said to me, as did a girl two years ago; "It was at the altar of the healing church that I came to accept Our Lord as my Saviour."

This girl has since married and has a baby. He has only been sick once, with a severe middle-ear infection. Crying and in obvious pain, she and her husband laid hands on him while the doctor was still at the house. "I've never seen anything like it," the physician said. "He quieted instantly and the following morning the infection had completely cleared up. Penicillin just doesn't work that fast."

This young couple, alternately baby-sitting one night a week, regularly attend healing services to pray for the sick. Infused with the Holy Spirit, they are powerful witnesses to God. Whenever I see them with their baby, the words of Isaiah (54:13) flash through my mind: "All thy children shall be taught of the Lord, and great shall be the place of thy children."

A girl of eighteen called me last week to ask prayers for her father, who was to undergo surgery for cancer the following day. "Yesterday when I was praying for him," she said, "I committed him to God, and I felt a flood of the greatest happiness I've ever known. This must be what is meant by 'Christian joy.' I've been singing around the house all day. Mother and Dad understand this, but other members of the family who have come on for the operation, sit around looking doleful, and say I'm callous and just don't care."

The morning this man was operated on, he received Holy Communion followed by Unction. The growth, smaller than anticipated, was discovered to be non-malignant.

Surely one of the greatest paradoxes of the healing ministry lies in the fact that although it emphasizes wholeness—healing of the body as well as of the soul—it has proved to be both the finest preparation and greatest comfort in time of death, both for the dying and for the bereaved.

Again and again people have come to me as did a recent young widow who had lost her husband under singularly tragic circumstances. "Words cannot express the comfort I have found in the healing ministry," she said. "I have found God as I have never known Him before. This does not mean there has been no grief or heartbreak or loneliness. There has. But never any bitterness or resentment, only an overpowering sense of His love and mercy and closeness. My life has been transformed, and I will never again be apart from Him." This woman has now organized a powerful prayer group.

God does indeed heal "the broken in heart, and bindeth up their wounds" (Psalm 147:3). And if the healing ministry enables those left behind to carry on with outstanding courage, fortified by a knowledge of the reality of the living God, so does the faith which so often produces life-saving miracles, prepare us to die.

Take the case of a woman who sought healing for her cancer-ridden body, through prayer and the sacramental healing rites. Shortly before she died she said to me: "I'll never cease to be grateful for what God has revealed to me of Himself. I know now that I am not in the process of dying, but of birth. He has planted in me a longing for Him which can't be satisfied here. All I *really* want is to see Him face to face; and all I honestly feel is joy that I soon shall."

For all of us the healing ministry is a peculiar mingling of certainty that God wills our wholeness, and knowledge that we cannot achieve *perfect* wholeness until we enter the Kingdom. Maybe it is not after all strange that the ministry of the life abundant should so ready us for our journey into the larger life. We go in faith, without fear, to an unknown place, perhaps, but not with an unknown Companion.

As the Christian faith is a unique compound of historical Event and revelation by grace, so is it a curious combination of mysticism and materialism. It is, as I have heard Bishop Pardue say, a system of merit and reward, by which we all unashamedly seek the greatest of all rewards—our salvation.

"Do this," says Our Lord throughout the Gospels, "and you'll get that." In no phase of the Faith is this more dramatically evident than in the healing ministry. Yet it is when "thy Father seeth in secret" that our motives in doing what we do are primarily spiritual gain and not material profit or physical benefit, that He most frequently "rewards us openly" (Matt. 6:4).

In praying for the sick we ask always for physical healing, but with increasing frequency I find myself praying over and above all else that the patient may know the Presence of God —for I have learned that the healing power of the Holy Spirit is almost always concomitant with the sense of His Presence. One without the other is possible but not probable.

A woman recently questioned me concerning the prayer the night that she was healed. "I was surprised," she said, "because you prayed chiefly that I might know the Presence and be given a knowledge of His love. The only reference you made to physical healing was to claim it, and offer thanks that it was done. What I don't understand," she went on, "is why this kind of prayer is intrinsically different from the ineffectual prayer we have offered for centuries with no real belief in healing."

The difference, I suppose, lies in the intent and the expectation. God hears our hearts. He knew that in mine that night lay the conviction that we cannot know His Presence or receive His love without a healing of our lives. We expect the most—an instantaneous healing. At the same time we know that the least that can possibly happen is the planting of the seed of healing in the spirit—a seed which in some cases grows slowly, but in all, grows surely, until, watered by continual prayer and thanksgiving, it flowers into a complete healing experience.

What phase of the wholeness we claim we may happen to emphasize in audible prayer under given circumstances, must be a matter of guidance, which I think is never withheld. In one case we may begin our prayer: "Lord, cleanse her of all resentment that thy healing light may penetrate every fibre of her being." In another: "Jesus, place thy healing Hand upon every organ of his body that he may be restored to the perfect health which is thy will." In another: "In the Name of Jesus, I rebuke this cancer"; or in another, where prayers are offered over a protracted period, we may change our emphasis from time to time, though never vacillating from the original expectation and intention of complete healing.

Take for example the case of a beloved relative of mine in his forties who became seriously ill with a heart ailment. In the beginning I emphasized his physical healing in my prayers, but as time went on I realized how greatly his condition was aggravated by apprehension and worry that he might lose his job. I then began to implore God to let this man know above everything else, the comfort and strength of His Presence.

Familiar with the healing ministry, the patient accepted without trepidation my suggestion that he receive Unction, and arrangements were made for anointing at his home between 8:15 and 8:30 P.M. on a certain evening.

An hour before the appointed time, the patient, a friend in the healing ministry (a medical doctor, incidentally), and I gathered together, praying alternately for the Presence of Christ and His healing hand upon the patient. When the priest arrived, we were enveloped in the Presence.

The patient knelt, flanked on one side by our friend, on the other by me. By prior arrangement, at the exact moment that the priest began the opening prayers, the participants in two local church healing services, were simultaneously receiving the laying on of hands on behalf of the patient; a number of Roman Catholics, and some ten healing clergy of different denominations were in prayer; a clergyman in Boston had halted a class he was conducting and asked their prayers; a doctor in Florida attending a conference glanced at his watch, and tapping his wife on the shoulder, they both went into prayer; and a number of prayer groups in Pittsburgh and Canton, Ohio, went into action.

We at home on our knees felt the tremendous impact of the spiritual power thus released—a power which seemed to steadily increase until it climaxed at the moment of the anointing.

When, after the blessing, the patient rose to his feet, there was about him that indefinable radiance we have so often noted in those who have felt the touch of Christ. In never-ending wonder, we claimed his healing, with only God knowing the extent of our humility and gratitude.

While it seems incontrovertibly true that those who participate in the healing ministry enjoy remarkably good health, your belief in the healing power of God obviously does not offer you an iron-clad guarantee that you will never be sick. It offers you something infinitely better: a constantly increasing receptivity to His love by which your hearts are recreated, and a closeness to Him through which you are spiritually reborn.

But Christ in the healing ministry as in every area of the Faith, meets you at the place of your current need and understanding; and if at first you need something more concrete to grasp than a "spiritual rebirth" presently implies, He, through the healing ministry, offers you a practical method of realizing His power—a practical means of combatting through Him, all dis-ease in your life—however trivial or however serious.

A young woman suffering almost total insomnia, sleeps, as a friend talks to her of the healing Christ, and kneeling at her bedside simply prays: "Father, let her sleep tonight."

A man in agony from cancer of the spine, receives surcease from pain as a minister anoints him with the prayer that "all thy pain and sickness of body being put to flight, the blessing of health may be restored unto thee."

A worried business executive feels the tension drain out of him as he prays: "Jesus, give me now your peace and your strength."

I think that few of us manage to live as fully in the Faith as we would like, or as we know we should—but He never fails to honor our efforts. As we gradually learn to "Cast all our anxiety upon Him, because He careth" (1 Pet. 5:7), we know a peace that is not of this world. As we claim His promises again and again, we come to rest serene in the knowledge that "With God nothing shall be impossible" (Luke 1:37).

As we experience the power of the Holy Spirit, we know the validity of His vow: "I will not leave you comfortless" (John 14:18). As we strive, no matter what the emergency to "Let not our hearts be troubled" (John 14:27), we find that they are indeed unafraid. An elderly woman to whom the healing ministry was relatively new, said: "I feel awful guilty about taking my medicine now. If I had the faith I profess, I shouldn't need it."

Perhaps not—but I think that not only should no one feel *guilty* about accepting medical help, but that to refuse it is presumption on our parts. God is the Author of all knowledge; to reject what He has given us seems to me a sin.

Your body is not yours. First it belongs to God, and then to those who love you, and you are obligated to keep it in as good condition as possible. God has given us both the physical and spiritual means to achieve wholeness. To repudiate either seems to me an affront.

"But," some protest, "*Jesus* healed without medicine." Yes, and so He does today. But He also said: "The sick have need of a physician" (Matt. 9:12); and nowhere in the Gospels does He negate the teaching in Ecclesiasticus (Chap. 38) where the patient is advised to call on the physician "whom God hath given that He might be honored in his marvelous works."

Seek God's help in every illness, but seek also medical care, praying that you will be led to a Christian doctor; praying that whoever he is that he will be divinely guided; and thanking God for *his* medical ministry of healing, which is God-inspired whether or not He is acknowledged.

"I will deliver thee, and thou shalt glorify me" (Psalm 50:15). As He works through men, He can deliver your body through medicine as surely as your spirit through Himself. But regardless of how you have been healed—through Him by medicine or by the direct intervention of the Holy Spirit, glorify Him in your life. If you do not, you are likely to find yourself relapsed again into illness. I have seen this occur with sufficient frequency to justify the belief that our praise and sensible witness involve a divine law which can be broken only at our own peril.

To live by the healing ministry is not to have all the difficulties of your life magically disappear, but it is to develop in you "the mind which was also in Christ Jesus" (Phil. 2:5). It is to make you, in Christ, a new creature (2 Cor. 5:17). It is to make you comprehend what St. Paul felt, when he said: "I glory in my weakness, that the power of Christ may rest upon me—for when I am weak, then am I strong" (2 Cor. 12:9, 10).

Persevere in this ministry as you do in prayer, and you will grow into a knowledge which can be imparted only by the Holy Spirit Himself—a knowledge so inestimably wonderful that no immolation of self seems too difficult, and no effort too costly, to procure it.

"Except the Lord build the house, they labor in vain that build it' (Psalm 127:1).

Live by all the great truths He died to give you, and He will build a finer edifice than you have ever dreamed, glorified by His continual healing Presence, and lit by His redeeming grace.

To live always in the light of Christ which surrounds you; to know always that you are enfolded in His love; to realize always that you are healed by His power, is to have your lives recreated in joy, transformed by the renewal of your mind and spirit, now unceasingly dedicated to the fulfillment of His perfect will (Rom. 12:2).

Chapter 19

the medical apostolate

A few months ago I talked to a group of doctors. After the meeting was adjourned several of us sat down together to discuss further the healing ministry, and within a few minutes we were joined by a clergyman who listened intently to the discussion for about half an hour. Then he volunteered: "You know, I've never really believed in spiritual healing, but after hearing you doctors talk, I'm beginning to think I was wrong."

This episode caused me to make a fascinating private conjecture. Could it be that the medical profession was going to end by being the promulgator of the full Christian Faith? This seems on the surface an absurd idea, but it nevertheless recurs to me fairly frequently when I meet not a few physicians who are more open-minded, outspoken and courageous about the whole subject than many of our theologians.

In speaking of this to one doctor who practices spiritual healing along with medicine, he vouchsafed: "You may be right at that—for while obviously it is the Church which has brought us knowledge of the healing Christ, it is dismaying to find so many of the clergy who are doing nothing to restore the ministry of healing. As physicians are in the best position, perhaps, to see the tremendous value of this ministry to their patients, it may not be too far-fetched to think that they may prove the persuasive force which will bring back this ministry into every church in Christendom."

While as yet comparatively few doctors are aware of, let alone practising, the healing ministry as such, the vital role of religion in health has never been so widely acknowledged by so many physicians, as in growing number they concede the co-relation of body and spirit in the total healing picture.

As a result of the work of the Institute of Religion in Texas, for example, a recent symposium of doctors and clergymen have proposed that departments of religion should be established as an integral part of every medical center. These men have recognized, as did the doctors affiliated with Houston's Medical Center, that the complete healing of the whole patient depends on spiritual as well as physical and mental therapy.

Dr. C. B. King speaks for many of his colleages when he says: "Medical men are recognizing to a greater extent that disease has in many cases a definitely moral and spiritual as well as physical basis. We are finding out that man is basically a spiritual being, and that the spiritual is actually dominant over the physical. Disease of the body is no longer generally considered an entity, but has its emotional and spiritual components. We doctors need help, and we turn to the healing Church; for there is nothing in our medical aramentarium to cope with spiritual illness."

The report of Dr. Edward Rynearson of Mayo Clinic confirms this last contention. He states that 70% of his patients have no need of pills or surgery, but they are genuinely sick, suffering from functional diseases for which examinations and laboratory tests can find no physical cause. Suffering real, not imaginary pain, these patients leave the doctor helpless because he can't solve their problems with a prescription or treatment of any kind.

Each month that passes seems to find more diseases, once considered purely organic, relegated to the psychosomatic area. The latest is cancer. In the Veteran's Administration Hospital in Long Beach, California, for example, tests have been conducted which indicate that tension-ridden, neurotic individuals cannot resist cancer as well as those who are well integrated and at peace. Time and again it was demonstrated that when tensions were lessened, the disease regressed; and that the patient's condition worsened in direct proportion to the increase in tension.

Dr. Eugene Pendergrass, Director at large of the American Cancer Society, has stated that he believes there is a definite cancer "personality." His theory is strongly supported by many medical men, including one of the world's outstanding gynecological-cancer surgeons, associated with New York's Memorial Hospital. As a result of this growing opinion, large grants for research in this field have been given.

In accepting the reality of psychosomatic disease, all accredited physicians have taken the first step by their acknowledgement of the enormous influence of the mind over the body. Many are now prepared to take the giant second step, which is to affirm the power of the spirit over both.

An eminent ophthalmologist was to see this power strikingly demonstrated in his practice not long ago.

A five-year-old boy suffered an accident to his eye which resulted in a perforated laceration of the cornea. Brought to the doctor's office on a Saturday morning with a prolapsed iris, the eye specialist and one of his colleagues agreed that surgery was necessary.

On Monday morning the surgeons were scrubbed and the patient anesthetized. When the protective eye pad was removed, the damaged eye was found to be completely healed. Aghast, the doctors questioned the parents, and discovered that the boy had been taken to a healing service on the previous day.

In the fullest sense of the word, the healing ministry includes the medical profession as well as the Church. When doctors and the healing clergy begin to work together on an extensive scale, the world will know a healing force of almost

inconceivable power. Such medical and clerical cooperation is
not a Utopian dream to be realized only in a dim and unfor-
seeable future. It has already begun.

In a constantly increasing number of hospitals, which include among many, Bellevue in New York, the Good Samari-
tan in Los Angeles and the Chicago Medical Center, the
clergy are now working side by side with doctors to heal the
sick, not merely to console the dying. As Chaplain Nathaniel
Whitcomb of Harvard Medical School states: "This is a ministry in which we can affirm Life, give hope and mark the beginning of that wholeness made possible through Our Lord."

Several years ago Dr. Charles P. Steinmetz, famous U.S.
scientist, had this to say: "When the day comes that scientists
of the world turn to the study of God and prayer and spiritual
forces which have scarcely been scratched, the world will see
more advancement in one generation than has been seen in
the last four."

There are signs that, on a very minute scale, this study is
now underway.

The conviction of more and more reputable scientists that
in healing there is frequently apparent the operation of a
supra-physical law, has resulted in the unprecedented amount
of religio-scientific research presently being conducted. Many
investigative committees, comprised of scientists, psychologists, clergymen and laymen, are at work, and their findings
have proved sufficiently impressive to warrant a government
financed project of religion and mental health in three of our
leading universities: Jewish (Yeshiva), Catholic (Loyola), and
Protestant (Harvard).

A number of conferences have been held in different sec-
tions of the country. The conclusion of the doctors attending
one of the most recent, was: "No cell of the body is impervious to or independent of, the spirit. The process at work
in the act of healing is the Holy Spirit functioning through
natural processes." At this same conference, a Freudian psy-

chologist converted to Christianity, observed: "If we keep God *outside* us, then I must agree with Freud that God is nothing but a projection of our father. But this is decidedly not so if God is encountered within one's being; and this, after all, is what Christianity is."

Not too many years ago, psychiatry and atheism were virtually synonymous, but no longer. In the new National Academy of Religion and Mental Health, six hundred clergymen, six hundred members of the American Psychiatric Association and six hundred psychologists, are working together in harmony and a mutual faith in God. As the eminent Vienna psychiatrist Viktor Frankl, comments: "Psychiatrists who ignore the spiritual side of mental disorders are like doctors who pretend a patient has no body above the neck."

The action and experience of a well-known psychiatric clinic are no longer unique.

About a year ago the clinic engaged a chaplain, not only for the patients, but also for the guidance of the interns and young psychiatrists. The minister was asked to leave a chair always vacant on either side of him in the dining room, so that young doctors could sit beside him if they wished. For over a month these chairs remained conspicuously empty until finally two young psychiatrists slipped self-consciously into them. From that day on they were never again vacant, and at the present time they are applied for in advance. There is hardly a luncheon period at which some doctor cannot be heard to say to the chaplain: "I think *you'll* do better with such and such a patient than I. Would you mind going to see him—or her?"

As the interest of many laymen in the healing ministry has been evoked by their personal need of healing, so have many doctors been converted to the healing Christ either through personal experience or personal observation of the healing power of God.

At a healing mission, for example, I recently met a physician who explained to me why he was there. It seems that a former patient, an alcoholic, whom he had been treating for a ruptured disc, and for whom surgery had been scheduled, was instantly healed through prayer and the laying on of hands, of both alcoholism and his back ailment.

"He called the office and told me his story," said the doctor, "but he did not come in to see me. Frankly I just didn't believe him, and I soon forgot all about the incident."

A few months later, the doctor was himself taken ill with pleurisy and pneumonia. Run-down physically from overwork, his condition became critical.

"I knew that I was dying," he told me, "and suddenly there flashed into my mind the story of my former patient. In desperation, I asked that he be contacted."

This was done, and within an hour the erstwhile alcoholic, accompanied by several members of his newly formed prayer group, was in the hospital praying at the bedside of the physician. He rallied immediately and dramatically, and was soon declared out of danger.

"I learned later," he said, "that my death certificate had already been filled out, awaiting signature. As a doctor, I knew the desperation of my condition, and the medically impossible rapidity of my recovery. Needless to say I believe now in the healing power of God, and am here to learn more of the ministry of healing so that I can benefit my patients."

Another doctor instantly healed of alcoholism at his church's healing service, prays now for his patients if they so desire, and not only urges them to attend local healing services, but often accompanies them. Another, who saw a patient so dramatically cured of cancer that he was convinced the healing could not be categorized as a "natural spontaneous cure," but was the result, rather, of God's power, has fitted up a prayer corner in one section of his office.

These men who combine spiritual healing with their medical practice achieve extraordinary results in their treatment of the sick. One surgeon, for example, reports that his death rate for seemingly "hopeless" cases is practically nil. An internist says: "I see now the need for Christian doctors who believe strongly in prayer—for I've discovered in my own practice that I am guided to make decisions and diagnoses which are far more apt to be correct than those I used to make solely on the basis of pragmatic medicine."

Three years ago a surgeon in a large city hospital was scheduled to operate on a woman for a malignant tumor, on a certain Wednesday morning. He examined her for the last time late Tuesday afternoon, and when he was ready to leave, the patient asked permission to have her prayer group come to the hospital later that evening while she was receiving the laying on of hands and Unction. The doctor, tongue in cheek, assented. Next morning she was wheeled into the operating room, and no evidence of the tumor was to be found.

Not long ago, in a church I was visiting, I met the doctor on this case. Knowing his former skepticism, I expressed my surprise at seeing him. "That healing experience made a Christian out of me," he grinned. "Never again will I doubt that God heals. I've joined the Church, and some wonderful things are happening in my medical practice."

It was a very similar experience which caused the chief of staff of another large city hospital, to see that a chaplain was engaged, and a cooperative medico-religious program set up in his hospital.

A professor in a medical school, at each of his classes, set aside time for the study of A REPORTER FINDS GOD THROUGH SPIRITUAL HEALING. Midway in the study, a beloved doctor on the staff of a local hospital became critically ill of cirrhosis of the liver. When everything possible had been done for him medically and his condition was termed "hopeless," a group of medical students began to pray for him, and he was apparently healed. Commented one of these young doctors-to-be: "Dr. DeLancey (onetime professor of internal medicine at the University of Buffalo) used to say, 'Whenever you enter a sick-room, enter with a prayer on your lips.' These words have real meaning for me now, and I'll never forget them."

Those doctors who are members of the Order of St. Luke unanimously attest to the tremendous impact upon their lives and their practice of medicine occasioned by their association with the Order.

General practitioner Dr. Louise Clark, a new member of the Order who had not yet attempted to combine the practice of spiritual healing and medicine, told me of an experience which occurred some three months ago.

A patient stricken with the most virulent type of polio, began to experience double vision—an indication that the optic nerve had been affected. Dr. Clark prayed with the patient, then left the hospital to make some house calls. On the way home, she felt a strange compulsion to stop by the hospital again, and lay her hand on the patient's eyes.

From the beginning of his illness, the boy had had a fluctuating fever, which reached its peak each day between three and four in the morning. After laying on hands, Dr. Clark returned home and called the parents, saying that she would arise next day at 4 A.M. and offer prayer for their son. This she did, and on the same morning at 10 A.M. a group of ten people received Holy Communion with special intention for the sick boy. That evening his eyes re-focused—and they re-focused *normal*—whereas before the illness he had suffered from reverse vision. A month later, the patient was playing football.

"This was the beginning for me," said Dr. Clark, "of a new and wonderful sort of medical practice. Both my patients and I have benefited immeasurably."

A few months past I met a well-known obstetrician on the first day of a healing conference, whose speakers included two psychiatrists. "They're the reason I'm here," he said. "I plan to make an abbreviated study of psychiatry in order to be of more help to my patients."

At the end of the conference several days later, I was surprised to see him being inducted into the Order of St. Luke.

"I've changed my plans," he said to me by way of explanation. "I want to learn all I can as fast as I can about the healing ministry. I see now that a normal, mentally balanced person can derive comfort and strength from this ministry far beyond any means at medicine's disposal."

The myth of the godless doctor is fast dying. Dr. Elmer Hess, past president of the American Medical Association, says: "I don't care whether you are a Catholic, a Protestant or a Jew, just so long as you believe in a Power greater than all the instruments of science at your command. The doctor has to be a man with firm convictions concerning a Creator."

Dr. Griffin Evans, internationally known surgeon, goes one step further. "Because man is made in His image," he says, "then the will of God and the love of God restores perfect form to those who *believe* and accept the 'Cup of Salvation.' "

Doctors unfamiliar with the healing ministry tend to associate it with the medically repugnant term "faith healing," which has become synonymous in medical minds with quackery. But as they overcome their initial misplaced antagonism and learn what the ministry of healing really is, more and more concur with the *New England Journal of Medicine*,* which in an editorial on the healing ministry, states: "—Axiomatic is the principle that it is the indivisible person who is to be restored to health.—The part that faith plays in the healing of the sick cannot and need not be experimentally demonstrable. On countless occasions it has been convincingly evident.—The term 'spiritual' need be viewed askance by no one, and least of all the physician, who should appreciate as well as any, the complicated pattern of personal existence and the

* The *New England Journal of Medicine,* Official Organ of the Mass. Medical Society, Vol. 259 No. 6, Aug. 7, 1958, p. 301.

varied and wondrous means through which health is often restored."

"With God all is possible," says Dr. Evans, "though we are far from understanding how."

The love and the mercy and the power of God is responsible for all healing, but the Spirit of God defies analysis. It took me a long time to come to this conclusion. A number of doctors have already reached it.

Chapter 20

"and they questioned, saying, what thing is this?"

Mark 1:27

Questions concerning the healing ministry fly thick and fast. Those which come to my attention are as often asked by interested clergymen as by puzzled laymen, all of whom are seeking a return to the Christianity of Christ.

Some of these questions I have endeavored to answer on the basis of experience, observation and actual case histories, within the context of this book. Others need enlarging upon, and a few are yet to be raised. Many answers must necessarily be conjectural; others must be personally experienced before they are understood; and still others must remain for us unanswerable, for none of us can pretend to fully comprehend the Mind of God.

Theodore Dreiser, a few months before his death, expostulated: "Damn it! Up to a year ago I lived all my life without God, and I might have had Him always."

This is very much the way I feel, yet in one respect alone, perhaps I am fortunate that for so long I knew so little of Him: I had no barriers of original misconceptions to break down. I am fully aware, however, of what must be the prodigious and sometimes frightening task, of eradicating the imprint of years of erroneous teaching concerning God and sickness and the fullness of His redemptive power. But regardless of background, I think that most of us will agree that the

Church is only sanctified by the Truth it represents, and its ministry only validated by the truths it promulates.

I have found that the critics of the healing ministry are invariably those who know the least about it; some because they have not as yet had the opportunity to learn, and other because they are chained to their teaching of many years' standing, and are unable to free themselves intellectually from their deeply inculcated prejudices. Their tendency is to ask questions, and refuse to listen to the answers; to make flat assertions, and close their ears to any rebuttals. However I have observed that time and again when eventually they *do* listen, they are gradually freed, and come to accept without reservation a basic premise of the healing ministry as it is of the entire Faith: that Christ is the same yesterday, today and forever.

There will always be a few people who, unwilling to have the status quo disturbed, merely quibble—but I have found that the vast majority are honestly seeking to learn more of the ministry of healing, and are asking earnest, thoughtful questions. Some of those most frequently voiced, I enumerate here, along with some of the theological criticisms occasionally heard. My attempt to reply to both is not undertaken presumptuously but with temerity, acutely sensitive to the possible pitfalls, and painfully aware that I am no theologian but only a convicted layman; whose conviction stems from what seems to me not only the unimpeachable scriptural authority for this ministry, but the overwhelming evidence of its theological validity.

(1) The contention is held by some that Our Lord never intended divine healing to extend beyond His own time; that His Commands were not issued to the whole Church, but only to the apostles.

I have searched diligently, but can find no scriptural evidence to support this claim. Was Philip of Samaria an apostle? Was Stephen? Was Paul?

The Gospels leave us in no doubt that not only were the Twelve appointed by Christ to heal, but also the Seventy (Luke 10:1, 9, 17, 20). That Jesus did not mean His healing to cease after the death of the last apostle seems clear, for twenty years later, Paul healed (Acts 19:12; 14:8, 10, etc.); twenty-six years after, the gift of healing was bestowed upon ordinary believers (1 Cor. 12:9); twenty-seven years after, St. James was to give us the pattern for today's healing ministry (James 5:14, 16). The frequent references to healing made by the early Church Fathers as long as three hundred years after Christ signifies that from the beginning of the Christian Church, healing was considered a natural part of her work and ministry.

In holding the contention that Our Lord's Commands were given *only* to the apostles, it is difficult for me to understand how anyone could then in good conscience attempt to teach any aspect of the Christian Faith. If His Commands were so confined, what are we doing with a Church at all? What is its function and what does its clergy actually believe? If they are consistent, they must feel that they are usurping prerogatives which do not rightfully belong to them—for no matter how ardent their discipleship, they cannot be numbered among the original twelve apostles.

(2) There are those who claim that although the gift of healing *was* originally given to the Church, it has been withdrawn.

This contention originated centuries ago, as an expedient explanation of the Church's diminished spiritual power.

Why is it held today in view of all the evidence to the contrary? Because there is still sickness? Then has His redemptive power also been withdrawn because there is still sin?

If we really believe He has withdrawn the healing gift, then we must also face the awful possibility that He has taken from us the promise of His salvation.

(3) The prayer of Christ in Gethsemane is frequently cited

as the crowning evidence that in all things, including sickness, we must be submissive to the will of God.

In the broadest sense, this is of course true. No Christian will ever deny that complete obedience to His will is the very heart of the faith—but let us be sure that we are submitting ourselves to God, and not mistakenly to evil, in His Name.

To attempt to equate Our Lord's experience in Gethsemane with uncured disease, seems to me to miss entirely the point of the Crucifixion. The suffering of Jesus was vicarious—of His own choosing and strictly according to His will, the fulfillment of which He had lived for and awaited for thirty-three years. He went to meet death, not death Him, so that He might overcome it. His sacrifice, freely offered for our salvation, the culmination of His destiny, is surely not to be misunderstood as an evil inflicted upon Him by God which had to be endured because it was God's will.

"Take away this cup," He said, in a plea that was not a plea at all. Scarcely before the words were spoken came His own reply: "Yet not what I will but what thou wilt" (Mark 14:36). He knew well His Father's will because it was His own.

To attempt to relate or apply this prayer to disease seems to me a monstrous distortion of its intention. It seems to confuse submission to the will of God, which Jesus knew and sought to teach us, with resignation to the enemy, whose identity Our Lord as clearly revealed to us in sickness as in sin.

(4) St. Paul's "thorn in the flesh" is often presented as the reason why we should not expect healing. "If God did not heal Paul, he certainly won't heal us," is the assumption.

There are as many conjectures as to the nature of Paul's "thorn" as there are theologians. One which I have heard voiced fairly frequently seems to me to make very good sense. It is based on what seems to be the unquestionable fact that Paul was healed. He was not, to be sure, healed immediately in response to his early supplication to God (2 Cor. 12:17); and it is suggested that his healing may well have been delayed because of his spiritual pride, jealousy and boastfulness, which is evidenced in his earlier writings (2 Cor. 11:11; 12:1; 12:11, etc.). Advocates of this theory point out that in his later writings, his change of heart and attitude are clearly apparent; and he stands revealed as the great Titan of the Faith, completely healed spiritually, and his "infirmity," whatever it was, distinctly a thing of the past (Gal. 4:13).

(5) Both those clergy and laity unfamiliar with the healing ministry cite its "dangers." One Churchman, for example, said to me: "The thing that bothers me most in the whole matter is that there are many truths involved here; and sometimes there are people who cannot hold many truths together, but see only one, and therefore are led to dangerous exaggerations."

This is a wholly reasonable statement and I fully recognize its truth, which is the reason why I continually emphasize the necessity of keeping the healing ministry within and carefully guarded by, the Church. It is the task of the Church to present the complete picture, and keep these truths in balance so that there will be a minimum of distortion and exaggeration in all areas.

I would point out further that there are many truths involved in the whole Christian Faith, and we do not eschew the Faith because many people are able to grasp only a small portion of them.

It is undeniably true that spiritual healing is subject to abuse, as is every other aspect of Christianity—but truth is still truth, and we cannot and must not murder it in order to obviate the possibility of its misapplication. The great and over-riding danger as I see it, is to kill the truth and thus the life, so that we find ourselves left with the Body of Christ without His Spirit.

(6) Fear of failure has appeared to me a consistently more common deterrent to the undertaking of a healing ministry than theological disagreement with its premise.

First there is the genuine fear that the failure of a believer to receive healing will have a disastrous effect on his faith.

The evidence to the contrary is overwhelming as anyone familiar with the healing ministry knows. All who are physically sick, whether or not their bodies are cured, can receive spiritual healing, which dwarfs by comparison any healing of the body.

A woman crippled with arthritis has sought God's healing power for years. She is still in her wheel chair, but she has converted as many to the healing Christ as any physically whole person I know.

A man is still bedfast, although he has received the healing rites for eleven years. His love for and knowledge of God are an inspiration to all who know him, including the clergyman who has faithfully ministered to him during the entire period of his illness.

The experience of the Rector of a large Episcopal Church is typical. "In my years of work in the healing ministry," he says, "I have yet to see anyone who has lost his faith because physical healing was not received—and this obtains also for the members of any family which has lost a loved one. I have never known such a family to be bitter because we prayed and built up false hopes. Instead, the loved ones tell me gratefully how the patient was without pain; how he grew discernibly closer to the Lord, and how the family was strengthened and comforted."

There is another fear which a number of clergymen have expressed, and this is the fear of personal failure—a sense of inadequacy in themselves; a feeling of apprehension that their own faith in what to them is a new ministry, may not be sufficiently strong.

To these the answer must be: "It is the Holy Spirit, not you, yourself, who is responsible. The success of your healing ministry depends not on your faith which will understandably be weak in the beginning; and not on yourself, but only on the Holy Spirit. Give Him a chance to take over this ministry for you. He will not fail to honor and bless it."

One particularly dubious minister who had spoken with me

some months before, said recently: "How right you were! Although I must confess that at the start I felt like the blind leading the blind, it was only a short time before people began telling me of the great spiritual benefits they had received from the services—and reports of actual physical healings soon began to trickle in. This ministry has already been mightily blessed, and I can only marvel that God has used me as He has."

(7) Many uninitiated clergymen fear hysteria and over-emotionalism in the healing ministry, but the experience of one such minister, who at this writing has a powerful ministry of healing within his own church, is common. He relates his first encounter with the healing ministry in action, when he attended not the usual church healing service, but a healing mission where emotion might be expected to run high.

"This mission at an Episcopal Church was attended by many hundreds of people," he says; "and I was surprised and greatly moved as I watched the devout stand for hours, reverently and quietly, waiting to receive the laying on of hands. I realized then that my fears had been ungrounded."

(8) Some claim that because the early Christians were of greater spiritual stature than are we, *they* were healed, but we are not sufficiently mature spiritually to receive God's healing grace.

The facts belie any such sweeping generalization. Especially noteworthy in this respect are those who are healed who seem to conspicuously lack both faith and spiritual understanding. Nevertheless, there is a strong element of truth in this contention, for there is no doubt that as we learn more of God we become increasingly receptive to His power.

(9) How much counselling is necessary in the healing ministry?

Most people need help from time to time as they seek the healing power of God. Those to whom this ministry is new, may well need instruction and "conditioning," as well as advice in what may be for them a new way of prayer.

Even those well-versed in the ministry need occasionally a penetrating and objective viewpoint in unearthing an unsuspected barrier to His power. I recall one woman, for example, in great need of healing. It was only after talking to her at some length that it became clear to me that although she wasn't aware of it, she actually didn't *want* to regain her health. She was revelling in her sickness as a means of gaining attention and satisfying her ego. We ceased to pray then for her physical healing, but asked instead a healing of the spirit for her that she might truly *want* the health which was eluding her. It was some time later before she could answer with an honest affirmative that all-important question: "*Wilt* thou be made whole?" (John 5:6)

The ideal combination is counselling and the healing Church, but I believe the former should be held to a reasonable minimum, remembering always that it is not a substitute for, but a tool of, the healing ministry. Otherwise it may become simply an indulgence and therefore an unproductive expenditure of time for the counsellor, and a weakening crutch for the supplicant.

I wish that prayer might mark the beginning and the end of all counselling sessions. While a chair across a desk is necessary, it seems to me no substitute for the floor under our knees.

(10) A number of clergymen in the liturgical churches, of which the Episcopal is one, are concerned over the propriety of receiving the healing Sacraments on behalf of others.

This is common and successful practice in the healing ministry, and "By their fruits ye shall know them" (Matt. 7:20). Nevertheless, I do not believe, as do some, that this question is necessarily obstructionist, bent on negating Christian experience on the grounds of a trivial technicality.

The Sacraments are never trivial, and I am sure that no one can be more concerned than I that they not be misused, and that the Church be protected from the danger of any possibility of heresy which might result from too-hasty innovations.

But to the precisionists, of whom I count myself one, I would call attention to the fact that we properly receive Holy Communion with Special Intention. When the laying on of hands is received "for" someone else, it is actually being received with special intention for the one who is ill. It's purpose is not an absent "treatment" for the one who is sick, but solely to bring him before God, and into a closer union with Him, that he may increase in receptivity to His healing power.

Some object that the imposition of hands as we pray for an increase of the Holy Spirit in ourselves, implies a repetition of Confirmation—a Sacrament which cannot properly be repeated. But in the healing ministry we accept the laying on of hands not to *receive* the Holy Spirit, which presumably we have already done through the Church in Confirmation, but to quicken Him within us. St. Paul seems to have this in mind when he says to Timothy: "Hence I remind you to *rekindle* the gift of God that is within you through the laying on of my hands" (II Tim. 1:6 RSV).

Further, if we are to be *really* precise, it seems to me we must differentiate between the laying on of hands and Holy Unction. Both are equally sacramental in nature, but the former is a sacramental *act*, while the latter alone is generally defined as one of the five lesser Sacraments. With this in mind, it is a virtually universal custom of the healing clergy within the Episcopal and other liturgical Churches, to lay hands on those who may be seeking healing for someone other than themselves. Sacramentalist as I am, I suspect that all of us may at times be guilty of splitting hairs, for Scripture strongly suggests that the early Christians, when circumstances warranted, received even *Baptism* by proxy (1 Cor. 15:29).

(11) "What about healings in the Jewish faith?" is a frequently asked question. "It's all the same God, isn't it?"

Some wonderful healings have occurred among the Jews, although they practise no healing ministry as such.

God healed long before the Word was made flesh—and He heals today even though that Word goes unheard and unrec-

ognized. But it is through Jesus that His healing has been
made available to the Church and to everyone—and it is when
our union with Him becomes sufficiently close, that we may
realize His promise: "He that believeth on Me, the works that
I do shall he do also; and greater works than these shall he
do" (John 14:12).

The question sometimes arises as to whether a Christian
clergyman, practicing Christian healing, should lay hands on
a Jew. This is a problem for each individual conscience; and
in no case which has come to my attention has the clergyman
refused when requested. My own feeling is, however, that to
seek healing through a Faith which one does not recognize,
in the Name of One in whom one does not believe, is apt to
prove futile.

(12) If faith is necessary to receive healing, what about the
sick who are unconscious—or children too young to know
what faith is?

The mere fact that a patient is not conscious, does not render ineffective or undiscernible to God the faith he holds in
his heart—nor the faith he retains intact in his subconscious.

As for children: it is not necessary that they "know" what
faith is—it is part and parcel of their being. Their enormous
receptivity to God's healing power; the extraordinary effect of
Baptism in time and again restoring a moribund infant to
complete health, is persuasive evidence of the validity of the
Church's teaching that faith is one of the theological virtues
received at Baptism. The pristine quality of this faith is apparently retained until, as the child matures, the increasing
encroachment of the world begins to weaken it.

(13) What about raising false hopes in gravely ill patients?

No doctor underestimates the therapeutic value of hope;
and most agree with Dr. Clair King, who asserts that through
hope and faith thousands now live who would otherwise have
succumbed to illness.

Anyone who has closely observed the healing ministry

knows that there is no such thing as "false" hope. One woman is healed of terminal cancer, and her hope for health is justified. Another dies, but she dies close to God; and her last words are: "Neither God nor the Church has failed me." She would be the last to say that her hope for wholeness had been misplaced.

(14) "How can I believe in the healing ministry when everyone is not healed?"

If you are like most, you "believe" in medicine—but what about the thousands who die despite receiving the best medical treatment? Does this fact prevent your using medicine?

Enough are cured by medicine and surgery to warrant your taking advantage of it even though many still die because of insufficient scientific knowledge. Likewise, enough healings of medically incurable disease occur through the healing ministry to keep us assured of God's will and power to heal; although many are not healed because of our insufficient knowledge of God.

(15) "But if some are healed, why isn't *everyone* healed?"

I don't know, any more than I know why all of us aren't better than we are, with the example of Our Lord before us, and His life in us. Yet I am convinced that His will for all of us is health as surely as it is for sinlessness; and when we fail to achieve either or both, the fault lies not with Him but with us.

As we have learned the necessity of following our doctor's orders if we are to be physically well, so we must learn the necessity of obeying God's Commands if we are to be whole. As our medical knowledge expands, additional lives are being saved each year, and so it is in the healing ministry: as our knowledge of spiritual laws increases, so do we with growing frequency experience God's healing power.

The healing Church has not attempted to build a theology on a few isolated phrases lifted out of scriptural context. "I am come that they might have life," He said, "and that they might have it more abundantly" (John 10:10). These are more than words. They constitute the theme which rings throughout the Gospels.

"Be of good comfort," He said. "Thy faith hath made thee whole" (Matt. 9:22). These are more than words. They convey the spirit which pervades the New Testament—the spirit of total salvation; healthy bodies as well as redeemed souls. As we come to recognize this, our "understanding is no longer darkened, and our hearts no longer blinded" (Eph. 4:18).

Christian experience has for centuries illumined and given His Life to the Church, and so it is today. To refuse to weigh and assess this experience; to suppress it, is to render the Church inert and dead, bereft of His Presence and stripped of His Power.

Chapter 21

the open door

A few weeks ago a neighbor discovered for the first time the healing ministry. On fire with his new knowledge, he exclaimed to me: "If people everywhere only knew about this thing, the whole world would be converted!"

This is what I, too, honestly if somewhat naively believed when I was first confronted with the fact of spiritual healing.

The knowledge that Our Lord lives as intimately among us today as He did among the people nearly 2,000 years ago; the fact that we can actually touch the Hem of His Garment and feel the impact of His Hand upon us, seemed to me then as it does now, the most incredibly exciting story of our time.

I was convinced that by telling this story; by presenting medically verified documentary evidence of His healing power, that no one could rationally continue to disbelieve. I was wrong; and I see now that there will always be those who "neither will they be persuaded, though one rose from the dead" (Luke 16:31). It has been my observation that their disbelief is most often founded not on intellectual or theological grounds, but on an adamant refusal to study the findings. Just as a verdict on a legal case cannot be rendered by a jury which has not heard the testimony, so no idea can be responsibly judged by those who refuse to consider the evidence.

I used to believe that as Our Lord commanded us to preach the Gospel to every living creature (Mark 16:15), so was the conversion of the world to be expected. I think that I was wrong. "Ye are the *salt* of the earth," He said (Matt. 5:13). He never said the "bread and the meat." And although "He is not willing that any should perish but that all should come to repentance" (2 Pet. 3:9), He never attempted during His earthly ministry, to *compel* anyone into belief. He proffered the truth, as must we; but when the Word fell on barren ground. He passed on to sow the seed in more fertile fields (Mark 4:16-20).

I used to deplore the fact that the healing ministry was not more universally embraced; but while it is my deep hope and fervent prayer that this ministry shall resume its rightful place as an intrinsic part of the total ministry of every church, I see now a possibility of danger were it to become over-popularized. As the conversion of Constantine "popularized" the Faith, so did it mark the beginning of the conventional, nominal and powerless Christianity which led to the decline of the Faith of the Church. It seems highly possible that the universal and thus inevitably unknowledgeable acceptance of the healing ministry, could lead once more to the withdrawal of the power of the Holy Spirit. Constant vigilance, careful teaching and the Church's maintenance of a proper balance between the spiritual and physical are safeguards which can avert this disaster.

While the central *facts* of Christianity are readily available, it has become more and more apparent to me that its inherent *truths* seem to be revealed only by grace.

"But why," asked someone not long ago, "is this revelation seemingly withheld in so many cases?" Perhaps St. Paul gives us the answer when he says: "The unspiritual man does not receive the gifts of the Spirit of God" (1 Cor. 2:14 RSV).

But this is not to say that the "unspiritual" can't grow in spiritual stature and increase in spiritual discernment. The extent of your desire for God is the determining factor of your growth and its only limitation; for as faith, great or small, is a natural consequence of this desire, so, I am convinced, is revelation merely an extension of faith. I believe with all my heart that to anyone who *wants* God enough, He will reveal Himself.

There are many like a woman I know who honestly believes she wants Christ, but does she? Or is her need greater than her desire?

"I wish I could believe that Jesus was the Son of God," she says dejectedly. She asks endless questions, yet is so preoccupied with her own questions that she never hears the answers.

"I've tried to read the Gospels," she says, "but I don't get a thing out of them." Yet as she reads she is so busy superimposing her arguments upon Our Lord's teaching that she cannot hear His voice.

"I've never found a church yet that has anything to offer me," she declares. Yet she never remains long enough in one to find out *what* it has to offer.

"Science is my God," she states with obvious pride (and how clearly I hear myself of a few years ago in her words). Yet science has repudiated the now distinctly old-fashioned theory that religious faith is incompatible with reason. The recent comment of an eminent doctor is neither rare nor iconoclastic today: "The world is governed by a system of Einstinian physics which medicine has not yet adopted," he says. "Behind the energy and vitality with which all things are vibrant, lies the Spirit of God."

I saw a man a month ago receive the laying on of hands. Deaf for twenty years, he hears today, although his eardrums were long ago destroyed.

I saw a woman three weeks ago for whom healing prayer was offered. Scheduled for surgery, her tumor is today dissolved.

Are such phenomena "impossible" scientifically? Not if the statement of one of our foremost scientists, Dr. Wernher Von Braun, is to be believed: "Science has found that nothing can disappear without a trace," he says. "Nature does not know extinction. All it knows is transformation."

The claim of skeptics that healing miracles are irreconcilable with science is not substantiated by modern science. It is rather a rationalization of our own unbelief in God, and His power and will to heal.

A great many devout people have said to me: "If only we were living during the earthly ministry of Our Lord it would be so much easier to have faith." I wonder if it would. The apostles' sense of union with their risen Lord *increased* as time went on. Their lives were transformed *after* the Resurrection, not before—and so it can be with us if we can realize that we are separated from Him in only one respect: by time. As He manifested Himself to His disciples through the breaking of the bread after the Resurrection, so does He make Himself as unmistakably known to us today through Holy Communion. He is more accessible now to more people than He ever was when He walked the earth. Through the Holy Spirit, His power is readily available, not to a mere handful of individuals as it was then, but to countless millions.

Twenty centuries ago, He was a highly controversial figure, little understood and revealed as Lord to only a few who had known Him at the longest, for several years. We have known Him now for many centuries; and we have 2,000 years of Christian experience behind us. Millions acknowledge Him as the Son of the living God, and more lives are being transformed by His healing power than ever before in history.

A man dying from an inoperable brain tumor, is marvellously restored—and witnesses now with the fervency of the apostles, to the power of God.

A woman suffering terminal cancer, is made whole—and works now with unimpeded vigor to advance the Kingdom.

A young boy crippled by polio, miraculously walks again— and commits his life to Christ.

A bereaved mother, her broken heart bound by His healing

Hands, is raised from her anguish—and lives now to His glory.

The other day someone remarked: "You know it's getting harder and harder to remain an atheist." For a moment I was cheered, but then I realized I had misunderstood; for subsequent conversation revealed that what the man had meant was that it was becoming easier and easier to be called a Christian.

"Admit that Jesus was a good man," he said, "and you're in." I'm afraid he's right. But although nowadays it may be easy to be *called* a Christian, it is as hard as ever to be one—or so it is for me. Sanctimonious religiosity has nothing to do with it; and the current tendency to think of God as a kind old man accessible to anybody on any terms, is a mawkish travesty of the Faith.

The Gospels make abundantly clear what is necessary for salvation—and that the road to the Kingdom is by way of Calvary. To try to evade its shadow is to become hopelessly lost. To envision this road as a limitlessly broad highway lit by neon signs flashing "Health, Wealth and Happiness" is to totally misapprehend the Way He has chartered for us.

"Strait is the gate and narrow the way," He said, "and few there be that find it" (Matt. 7:14). Believing His teaching as well as His promises, I cannot simultaneously believe that somehow and regardless, everyone will automatically wind up in heaven.

As I have come to understand it, Christianity seems a far cry from an effortless, rocking-chair sort of religion. It is not an emotion-drenched, sentiment-soaked state of euphoria, but a challenging, blazing, transfiguring and sometimes consuming, power. While the Faith is filled with joy, it is by no means a soporific; while it gives ineffable comfort, it is never comfortable; while it unquestionably brings the "peace which the world cannot give" (John 14:27), it is at the same time an unremitting battle. "I have not come to bring peace, but a sword," He said (Matt. 10:34 RSV), and the wielding of this sword requires unflagging effort, energy and stamina.

It is not a religion for those who are desperate for easy answers, but for those who hunger for the truth. It is not for those who seek nirvana, but for those who seek the Christ—and it is not for those who *seek* Him only—but for those who know He must be served as well as sought. It is not for those who seek a panacea for all tribulation, but for those who know that without the Crucifixion there can be no Resurrection.

Spiritual healing is for many of us perhaps the most difficult aspect of the Faith, for it is the least amenable to compromise. The world is filled with purely nominal Christians, but it is impossible to be a merely nominal advocate of the healing Christ. This is a purely demonstrable faith which cannot be masked by vague ambiguities or obscured in a maze of ecclesiasticism.

Sharp still in my memory is my first encounter with the unveiled Gospel of Christ, proclaimed, believed and practised —the first time I saw a goiter instantaneously disappear; a cancerous sore dry up before my eyes; a blind man with his corneas destroyed, see; a deaf woman with no eardrums, hear.

Ever since the healing ministry swam into my ken and I began to grasp its significance, I have been perpetually on my knees, figuratively speaking—and literally on them much of the time. But it is not the miracles of physical healing which keep me there. It is the knowledge that Christ lives.

The moment without parallel in any life must be as it has been in mine, that in which we first realize and then experience, the living God. You suddenly know beyond the shadow of any doubt that in Him lies the answer to all things for all men, forever—that to possess Him compensates for the loss of the whole world. That which long ago began as an indefinable restlessness—an unknown longing—is at last identified, and becomes the reason for your life.

A clergyman interested in instituting healing services in his own church, recently attended those in another to see how they were conducted. Later that same evening he said to me: "An extraordinary thing happened tonight. I was healed of doubt—a doubt I never knew I had until I arose from the altar rail conscious that it had gone."

A young business man was to say to me a few weeks ago: "My favorite hymn is 'Breathe on me Breath of God.' I finally discovered what this meant the other night when I received the laying on of hands for the first time. I actually *felt* His Breath. An experience like this can't be put into words. It's enough to say that it changes your whole life."

The Tidings of Great Joy—the irrevocable knowledge that God lives—comes to multitudes as in no other way, through the ministry of healing.

To our endless supplication, "Lord have mercy upon us," we know His instantaneous response: "Let not your heart be troubled. As the Father hath loved me, so have I loved you: continue ye in my love" (John 14:1, 15:9).

To our eternal cry, "Lord, save or I perish," we know His swift assurance: "There shall be not a hair of your head perish, for I the Lord thy God will hold thy right hand, saying with thee, fear not; I will help thee" (Luke 21:18, Isa. 41:13).

Enveloped in His love and cloaked in His mercy, and now supremely confident of both, the once-muted pleas of desolate hearts; the once tentative beseeching of pain-racked bodies are transformed into a triumphant canticle: "Heal me, Lord, and I shall be healed. Save me, and I shall be saved" (Jer. 17:14). Our healing—our salvation—is actualized in the healing Church.

The life of Our Lord, from His Conception to the Ascension, is a miracle. To the Christian world the Resurrection is the most significant day in all history—for it was the empty tomb—the victory of Jesus over death—which was to give men for all time their "sure and certain hope"; and fill with faith the hearts of endless generations to come.

But for many of us, as for me, there is a peculiarly personal sort of miracle involved: it is not only that He died and rose, or even that He was born—but that at last we *know* it; that each morning we may awaken, as we go to sleep at night, in the grateful awareness of His continuing Presence.

"Is it nothing to you, all ye that pass by?" (Lam. 1:12) With a thankfulness beyond the telling and a joy beyond expressing, we can finally answer "Everything."

A few years ago, Elwood Worcester, erstwhile rector of Emmanuel Episcopal Church in Boston and pioneer in the restoration of the healing ministry as we know it today, was to predict that the revival of this ministry would have as dynamic effect on the Christian world as the Reformation. There is no little evidence that his prophecy will be fulfilled.

A brilliant electrical engineer underwent surgery in which a vital part of his brain was removed. Medically doomed to live out the remainder of his life as a human "vegetable," the healing ministry was to come to the attention of his wife. His name was placed on several prayer lists, he received Unction at regular intervals over a period of months, while during the same period his wife attended healing services, receiving the laying on of hands with special intention for him. Gradually this man began to function normally, until today he is able to be back at work.

A man dying from an incurable heart ailment and bedfast for two years, insisted upon personally attending a healing service. Carried in on a stretcher, he received the healing sacraments. Within a month he was able to resume his duties as vice-president of an internationally known organization.

A young girl, diagnosed by five doctors as the victim of an incurable disease, was instantly healed by the power of God released through prayer. Her recovery so astonished her physicians that they requested that she submit herself to some sixteen doctors for examination. The consensus was that her healing was some sort of "miracle," not explainable by spontaneous regression.

Cases such as these mark the end of the beginning; and I see the start of a chain reaction of healing which is gaining in momentum, and must ultimately set the world on fire.

I have come to believe that religious experience constitutes for each one of us the infallible evidence that God is—and yet I become daily more convinced that it is through spiritual healing that so many of us are first led into this experience. Two thousand years ago, Jesus united Himself with us. Today we are able to unite ourselves with *Him* in a unique and wonderful way through the ministry of healing; and in this reconciliation, we "shall be filled with the knowledge of the glory of God, as the waters cover the sea" (Hab. 2:14).

What once appeared to me as flagrant contradictions in the Gospels, now seem inconsistencies which are paralleled in all of life. As I have remarked throughout this book, the healing ministry, as is the entire Faith, is filled with paradoxes—and the final great paradox seems to me this: To pray for Christ's healing here and now—and yet to know that "If in this life only, we have hope in Christ, we are of all men most miserable" (1 Cor. 15:19).

To pray for the preservation of physical life—and yet to know that death is the gateway to everlasting life; and He "shall be magnified in my body, whether it be by life or by death" (Phil. 1:20).

To strive to be made whole through Christ—and yet to know that complete wholeness on this earth must always elude our grasp.

To fight sickness in His Name—and yet to accept death if it comes, in the certain knowledge that it is not death to die, for "to die is gain" (Phil. 1:21).

Comprehension of this paradox comes by grace, as by grace comes our willing acceptance. This is the ultimate benediction bestowed upon us by a merciful God.

A recent bereavement has vindicated everything I have believed and intuitively felt about the healing ministry. Through the vision of the healing Christ, I and many like me, have embarked on the first lap of the journey from faith into knowledge—a journey which can only be completed when we come into the nearer Presence of God.

"The time cometh when I shall show you plainly of the Father," he said (John 16:25); and that time seems near at hand as through the healing ministry we catch glimpses, with increasing frequency and startling clarity, of His glory.

When my first book on spiritual healing appeared five years ago, a reviewer commented that it was of particular value because it was written by an outsider—someone not intimately involved with this ministry. This book then, by necessity, must lack that specific value, for the healing ministry is no longer a casual interest. It has become for me a way of life; the healing Christ the strongest certitude I know.

Led to the brink of belief by my mind's conviction, I was to take, with no little trepidation, that final step of faith—a step which I discovered was not a step in the dark, but one into incredibly brilliant light. It has at last become clear to me that none of us are significant apart from our relationship with God; that at all times and in all things it is not I "but the Father that dwelleth in me, He doeth the works" (John 14:10). This was an extremely difficult lesson for me, and I suspect for many, to learn.

Once having known the healing ministry, one cannot live without it—for he who has known the light can never willingly step back into darkness; as he who has once known sight can never voluntarily retreat into the world of the blind. Least of all can anyone who has known the healing Christ ever turn aside from His outstretched Arms.

Spiritual discipline is no doubt easier for some than for others. For me it has often seemed unbelievably difficult, but I have at least learned what He meant when He said: "He that followeth me shall not walk in darkness, but have the light of life" (John 8:12).

I think no one understands better than I the rigors of attempting to live by the full Christian Faith. But I am equally certain that no one has been privileged to more completely realize the fullness of its power and the radiance of its glory.

"Why standest thou afar off, O Lord?" asks the Psalmist (Ps. 10:1). Through the healing ministry we now recognize His nearness.

"If you knew me, you would know my Father," Jesus said (John 8:19). Through the healing ministry many of us have come to know Him; and "we speak that we do know and testify that we have seen" (John 3:11).

"I give unto you my power," He said (Luke 10:19). Through the healing ministry we see that power in action.

But He has given us more than knowledge and more than power. He has given us Himself—and this is the transcendent miracle.

"Behold, I have set before thee an open door" (Rev. 3:8). I see in the healing ministry that door which no man will ever again be able to close. We have only to walk through it now to find the healing Christ—and in Him, the Kingdom.

INDEX

213